The **19** Cent Millionaire

MARIAN WARDLAW

authorHOUSE®

AuthorHouse™
1663 Liberty Drive
Bloomington, IN 47403
www.authorhouse.com
Phone: 1-800-839-8640

First published by AuthorHouse   5/27/2011

ISBN: 978-1-4634-1305-7 (sc)
ISBN: 978-1-4634-1308-8 (hc)
ISBN: 978-1-4634-1306-4 (e)

Library of Congress Control Number: 2011908212

Printed in the United States of America

**To
Sydney,
Hunter,
and Dorothy.**

~~~

**May you always know how much I love each of you.
Thank you for your love, support, patience,
and constant faith in me.**

~~~

Preface

One fall day, on my way to pick up Dorothy from day care, I went by the outside teller machine at my local Regions Bank to find out my exact checking account balance. I knew I didn't have much money in there and I had just about become resolved to the fact that my life was a crazy cycle of "borrowing from Peter to pay Paul," as I heard the term used many times in my life. As I read the number on the front of the ticket, however, I had no idea how my account was that low, nor how that day would change the course of my life forever. As my heart sank, I had to look through tears to read the faint number on the ticket again that was now trembling in my hand. The number I saw, $.19, stared hauntingly right back at me. Had I not been seated in my car, I might have fallen over or passed out. But with no one looking, I began to sob uncontrollably. I could feel every muscle in my body tighten up and I felt like such a failure. Here I had 3 children counting on me to keep our lives afloat and all I had was 19 Cents in my checking account, and no savings. I had secured a great job, but everything, and I mean everything, either went to day care, rent, car, utilities, and then we'd see if we could eat. I was already living so "close to the bone" I couldn't see how I could live any closer. I felt so alone and my heart literally began to ache.

After I couldn't cry anymore, my mind began to race around in circles trying to make sense of all of this and I feverishly began trying to figure out a plan of action. I'd come too far to admit defeat now and quitting just wasn't an option. In an instant, however, completely out of nowhere, and what I have come to know as The Holy Spirit, a vivid thought came to me......It was as clear as a bright, sunny day. I said out loud to myself, "One day I am going to make it out of this hole and I am going to write a book to show other women how to stay positive in the face of adversity." Again, I have no idea how or why that particular thought came to mind, but it was crystal clear. I was to write a book. Then, almost as immediately as the idea had come to me, so did the name of the book: The 19 Cent Millionaire and I never once waivered on that title. I said aloud again, "I am the 19 Cent Millionaire." "Wow," "Big deal, right?" But even in those moments of despair and flat out panic, with only 19 cents to my name, somehow I still felt like the richest woman in the world.

Of course, realizing that I felt this immense calling to write a book one day didn't seem to do me any good right then, nor did it help me put food on the table or pay any of my bills. But believe it or not, what it did do was give me a purpose, a goal, and a mission. If nothing else, it gave me something tangible to sink my teeth into and it made me think that I was to do something special with my life that could possibly help someone else. And more than that, it kept me from giving up on myself. Almost instantly, I was invigorated with hope.

Needless to say, the dynamics of our story have changed greatly over the past 7 years and many new chapters have been added. But the underlying fact is that each moment: whether happy, sad, or somewhere in between, has molded me and my children into the people we are today and has taught each of us many valuable, life-changing lessons.

In the 7 years it has taken for this book to come to life, I have met many people who have inspired me to keep going on my quest when I became discouraged, from time to time. Out of the clear blue, it always seemed, whether it be family or friends, or even complete strangers, I would hear someone else's story and remember the promise I had made to myself, and to my children, to see this project through to fruition. I thank God for placing these particular people in my life and on my path, so that my own hope could be restored and so that I could pass on my knowledge to possibly change one person's life for the better. And as I said to myself some 7 years ago, if I can help just one person, I will feel that my efforts will have been worth the effort and a complete success.

Therefore, it is my hope, for all of you who read my book that you may find something in the pages within that you can use in your own life, or something you can use to help someone else you know as you continue down your path. It is my wish, too, that those who have ever thought themselves too far gone for a positive change or felt themselves a victim, that you will receive encouragement and hope to know there is always a way out and you can become the victor. There is always hope! So I thank you for choosing my book to read and I welcome you, as you open the pages of my heart, to also open your own heart, your mind, and your spirit.

Enjoy~

Contents

Chapter 1 Head over heels

Out of the corner of my eye, I saw a blur of gold just before I felt the impact. Our van was hit with such force that the car instantly began to flip. I don't really know what happened next or how long it took; but eventually the car came to rest on all four wheels. After what seemed like an eternity of squealing tires and the pounding and scraping of metal on pavement, all I could hear was the crying of my children.

I looked back to where Sydney, my two-year-old, was supposed to be. I saw her still buckled in her seat, but obviously scared to death. She was crying at the top of her lungs and was looking frantically around for me. I looked to where I had last seen Hunter, my four-month-old. Luckily he was still in his car seat, but his carrier top covered him completely. With intense fear, I slowly lifted the cover off of his body. No blood. No obvious injuries. No deafening silence. I immediately saw this as a good sign.

Shaking, I looked around the car. Our groceries: cans of soup and green beans, lay in the seats, the floorboard and on the dash. Not one of the van windows was still intact. My eyes then focused on a pencil that had been driven through the one piece of the windshield that still hung in the frame. Having difficulty moving about, I slowly unfastened my seat belt and began to try to comfort my children. The impact of the initial hit came on my side of the car and I realized I could not open my door. It was then that angels in the crowd of people, who had obviously witnessed the wreck, began to come to my aide and try to get my door ajar. I thought I heard them saying that the van had flipped three to five times, but its final resting place was on all four wheels. I couldn't help but sense that God had personally offered His hand to protect us all from what was sure death.

The 16-year-old who had run the red light was unharmed and came to check on us. When the paramedics arrived, they examined each of us before transporting us to the hospital to make certain we had no internal injuries. But how do you really know what is wrong with a four month old or a two year old who has just learned to talk? Those minutes, that became hours, were agonizing.

The accident was a turning point in my life. In a marriage that was already traveling down a rough road, the accident proved to be something of a prophecy of my life over the next few years: blind-sided and hurling head over heels, but with God's grace, landing on my feet.

Chapter 2 The little concrete house

"Has this ever happened to you? You are washing your face and suddenly you do not recognize the woman staring back at you. "Who is this?" you asked the mirror on the wall. No reply... Psychologists call this phenomenon the "displacement of self," and it usually occurs during times of great stress... But what's wrong? What is this great sadness we cannot name? Perhaps the heart of our melancholy is that we miss the woman we were meant to be.... Listen to the whispers of your heart. Look within."

-Sara Breathnach,
Simple Abundance

The house we lived in at the time of the accident was on the main road and made of concrete blocks. It wasn't in great shape when we first moved in, but it was right up the road from my in-laws; and we were grateful for a place to call our own. I had painted and cleaned, planted flowers and did what I could to make it a cozy home, all the while I was pregnant with my second child and toting Sydney around. My husband was a skilled craftsman, but work on our house - like time with us - fell to the bottom of his priority list.

After the accident, I had no car, no access to a phone, and very little contact with the outside world. My days at home with my children were very simple, but I came to like it that way. At first, I welcomed the quiet days at home curled up on the couch reading with them. They loved Barney and would march around the house or ride their little trikes singing Barney songs. They were wonderful entertainment for me and I marveled as I watched them grow and develop. Sydney would help me cook and clean, and we would laugh with sheer joy as we made messes while we mixed cake batter or made a meal. Hunter fascinated me with the way he explored his world. Together, we celebrated every wonderful moment: we made tents with blankets over the dining room chairs, played hide and seek, sang and danced together. Those days were priceless to me and fed my spirit so that I was able to endure what nighttime would bring.

I used to call my husband the hardest working man in town because I thought he was out trying to make a better life for us. He was never home. But I learned, bit by bit, that he was actually out gambling and drinking away the little money we did have. With no phone, I never had a way to call or contact him and he never came by to check on me either, so I worried about whether or not he was safe. I made excuses for him and his whereabouts so that the children could be proud of their dad. When he would finally come home, very late each night, I would carefully watch the way he got out of the truck. A part of me died every time I saw the shadow of our windows move across the wall as he pulled his truck into the driveway. I was always relieved that he was okay and that he hadn't hurt anyone, but also overcome with dread, and yes, even intense fear.

I'd stand in the living room and watch him as he staggered up to the front door. By the reflection from the porch light I would try to read his face and determine if he was going to be the happy drunk this time or the angry drunk. I wanted to keep peace in my home, so I tried to be ready for him to avoid any conflict. One night he would yell at me for opening the door too soon. The next night, I opened it too late. The food was always too hot or too cold, too salty or not salted enough. Many nights he threw his plate across the room, food and all, and told me to clean up the mess and bring him something suitable to eat.

Most of his threats against me were empty, but I honestly had no way of knowing which ones he would deliver on. He seemed to enjoy having such control over me and making me wonder when my punishment would come. As soon as he sat down on his favorite couch in front of the television he would begin to belittle me. One night, in one of his screaming rages he yelled, "I wouldn't sleep too hard if I were you. I'll come pi-s and sh-t on your head." Many nights he made me do degrading things I didn't want to do. I could not fight back because I was afraid for my life and the children's if I didn't do exactly what he said. So through many tears, I did everything I could to protect my children.

I learned a lot in those horrible nights. When you're flat on your back and you cry, your tears run down from the corner of your eyes and through the curves and channels of your ears. They soak your hair, and they leave you messier than crying when you are standing on your feet. It's hard to breathe with someone on top of you, especially someone you don't want to be there or who you feel doesn't deserve to share such an intimate space with you. You want to scream, but you know you can't because you don't want to wake your children and make him angry. Through the nightmare of abusive sex with my own husband, however, I learned that I could endure things no one should ever have to face. I learned that I was stronger than I ever imagined and that I would never allow him to control my spirit.

I may never know how deeply those nights affected me. Did they make me separate who I am spiritually from who I am physically and sexually? What reward in that little concrete house made that price worth paying?

Sleep never came easy. When it did, it was filled with nightmares. One night, in the silence that came when the alcohol overcame him and finally delivered me from his torture, I had a reassurance deep in my soul that let me know I was not alone. I lay in the bed and tried to be perfectly still. I strained to hear the voice that spoke inside me: "you are just as worth saving as your children."

Chapter 3 Tall and broken

The visits to the doctor following the wreck revealed that our bodies would heal, but we would each need variations of treatment in the meantime. Seat belts had saved all of our lives, but it would be some time before any of us felt comfortable in a car again. For months, even years following the wreck, I had excruciating neck pain and nausea. My mother-in-law or my husband would take me to see a brother and sister team of chiropractors there in our little town. Dr. Mack and Dr. Beth showed me such kindness that I often suspected they knew my deep, dark secrets. They took extra time with the children to make certain that the accident had caused no long-term problems. They talked to me. They listened to me. They befriended me. They gave me wonderful care. "Dr. Mack's" wife once gave me a book, *Simple Abundance*, which I read every day for years and have shared with many friends since.

During my days at home with the children, I would read the devotional book and pray for strength. I prayed for God to show me what I looked like through His eyes. I struggled trying to discern what God wanted me to do. I knew we had survived the accident because of His wondrous protection, and I felt His comfort with me in the living hell that my home became following the accident. I also knew that God hated divorce; and to be honest, I wondered if I had allowed myself to get into this mess as a form of punishment because of the failure of my first marriage. So many questions and not enough answers.

It was only three months after my divorce from my first husband that I met the father of my children. He was tall and charming. I was tall and broken. Hurting people make bad decisions and for whatever reason, I gave myself to this man too quickly. Maybe those of us who fall in love too quickly are just trying to give someone else what we ourselves long for so deeply. Maybe some people are predators and they smell the wounds of hurting people and the wounded become prey. I told myself that I was being cautious, but I disregarded warnings from my parents and brother who loved me and only wanted what was best for me. They say that "love is blind," but in hindsight, there were warning signs so I know I was not blind. Rather, I saw glimpses of his character flaws and dismissed them because something inside me needed to be with him. I had always looked so deeply for the good in others that I would not allow myself to see what was right in front of me. His father was a wonderfully, loving man and I knew he had to have that kind of love inside him somewhere. I could feel that I loved him, and I know how this sounds, but I thought I could love him enough to change him into the man I knew he could be, or that I wanted him to be. I honestly just wanted to be loved.

Friends who have been involved in recovery programs like NA or AA tell me that the programs advise people to postpone any new romantic relationship for at least a year after their last drug use. The idea behind that advice is that the euphoria of a new relationship can create the same "high" as their drug of choice. That high separates the addict from the real reason he or she used drugs in the first place. So, instead of doing the very hard soul-searching work that will help them grow and stay clean, they have a new drug which, of course, eventually fails them. Getting involved so soon after my divorce probably was not the best idea, but I have three beautiful children from that relationship and I count them as my greatest gifts and life's ultimate blessings.

It some ways, it was easy for me to deceive myself about my husband's potential. His parents, a gentle caring Southern couple, moved as one person. They had built a life together by a heart-felt respect for one another and gentle humor that helped them skate over the rough spots that are a part of every relationship. My husband's father, "Papa Bill," smelled of cigarettes, the starch in his shirts, and the hard work that had built his business and fortified the respect the community placed in him. He was an electrician; and all over town, people turned to him and casually handed him the keys to their homes without hesitation. If you needed a breaker replaced or new wiring throughout the house, you could trust Bill for quality work at a fair price. He had built his business one faithful relationship at a time. He loved the simple joys of life: time with his wife, his grandchildren, and the wonderful rest that comes at the end of a good day's work. But he was not a "simple" man. He was very smart and invested in property and saved his money so that he was able to care for his family. His wife, "Mama Dot," was his perfect counterpart. She, like many Southern women, waited on her husband hand and foot when he was home, even though she had worked a full day herself. Mama Dot worked at the local water company and was as well-known and well-liked as her husband. From the day I met them, I loved them, and I could tell they loved me.

My husband's son from a previous marriage sealed the deal. He was six years old when his dad and I started dating. He had a wonderful relationship with his mother but he still willingly welcomed me into his life. I longed for children of my own, and the hours spent listening to his stories filled my heart to bursting and erased away any concerns I had about his father's occasional selfishness. I often thought my husband's family hoped I was going to be his "savior," in a manner of speaking. I did think I could change him and help him become a better man. I kept my mind focused on the good times and tried not to think about his temper, his drinking, and what eventually became abusive behavior. I took the "crumbs" he dished out and thought it was love.

What I know now that I did not know then was that we teach people how to treat us; and unless we expect the best, we very rarely will get it.

Chapter 4 My angel...finally!

Before the wedding, my brother came to me at the urging of my father. He took me aside and listed specific reasons that they were against me staying with this man. I saw their advice as meddling and confidently told him that he needed to look for the good in others. Never in my wildest nightmares could I have imagined what lay ahead of me, but my family seemed to see things I did not.

After our wedding, we lived in my parent's lake house. While we lived there, God blessed us with Sydney, the beautiful and perfect baby I had always dreamed of. My husband was a wonderful birth coach. I still remember thinking "if he could only be 'out there' the way he has been 'in here'."

For years, I had ached for a child. My first husband's decision to postpone having children; and my feeling of urgency in beginning our family had started the divide that eventually resulted in our divorce. I knew I was going to love my babies, but as they handed this miraculous child of God to me, I was completely undone by my love for her. As much as I had prayed for her, I still could not have anticipated or imagined the powerful feelings that rushed over me. I watched my husband as he held her so tightly and said "I'll always take care of you." Even now, I believe that he meant that promise as he whispered it in Sydney's ear. It just wasn't meant to be. I had hoped that he would stay with us that night. I did not want to break the spell that seemed to surround our hospital room. This was the way it was supposed to be: the three of us together.

That night, I stayed awake in my bed examining every square inch of Sydney. I nursed her, sang to her, and continuously smelled and brushed her precious, new baby head. You know the smell: the same smell that is as distinct as that of a little puppy's breath. Two smells you just don't ever forget. I was simply overcome with joy! I changed her tiny diapers and talked to her about how much fun we were going to have as she grew into a young girl and then a woman. Mostly, Sydney slept, but sometimes she would open her eyes and try to focus on my face. It was as if she was saying hello to me and telling me how glad she was that I was her mom. Her dad disappeared into the night as soon as the new wore off of the experience. I suppose he thought it was his "just due" to celebrate the birth of his daughter with the guys at the local bar instead of with me. Alone with Sydney, my heart was broken, but I had a whole new reason for living that would give me strength I never knew I had.

Chapter 5 Family

All fathers are invisible in daytime; daytime is ruled by mothers and fathers come out at night. Darkness brings home fathers, with their real, unspeakable power. There is more to fathers than meets the eye.

-Margaret Atwood, Cat's Eyes

Sometimes for weeks at a time, the children and I were forbidden to go outside the concrete house. I learned later that when he owed someone a lot of money, my husband needed us to hide out. He felt that if anyone saw us and stopped by that I would learn things he didn't want me to know. Occasionally though, the children and I were given permission to go outside. I would sit on the front steps and watch them run and play. From my porch I could watch the cars go by. I could see families going to dinner together. An evening out in public as a family is such a simple thing to most; but to me, it seemed like the makings of fairy tales. I would sometimes imagine that my husband would come home early and surprise us by taking us all out to eat. Even a picnic we carried from home would have been nice, just to be out together, like the other families I saw around me.

My dad had always been proud of his four children and seemed to love to show us off. My parents had a miscarriage on their first try for children, but in the next few years, they had my sister, Susan, and my brother Dave. Their plan was to stop there, but soon found out they were expecting my sister Nancy. She was always known as the "surprise of the family," and when I was born some four years later, I got the distinction of being called the "shock of the family." I was given this name in all due respect, of course, for I did feel their love for me, but it did stick and was the brunt of many jokes over the years. All in good fun, though, all in good fun.

Dad was from Abbeville, SC; and mom was from Birmingham, AL. Mom's claim to fame was that she was the longest baby born in Birmingham at that time. She was 26 inches long and grew to be a tall, beautiful woman by the time she caught my dad's eye across a crowded dance floor.

I later found out that my dad, who was painfully shy at the time, had broken in on her dance just to meet this tall beautiful woman with the best looking legs he had ever seen. They didn't see one another until months later and their next date was a function at church. One of the ladies sitting in a pew close by commented on the fact that they made such a handsome couple. Her intuition proved correct because 4 years later, after my dad graduated from dental school at Emory, he and my mom were married on June 1, 1952. It was then they moved to Anderson, SC, to begin their new life together, start a family, and open his dental practice.

Dad was home with his family almost every evening except for when he was playing chess with his buddies or working on clocks. He had lots of activities, but was actively involved in every aspect of our lives. His passion was tennis and handball in my younger years, but when his children started swimming competitively, he encouraged us to follow our hearts and to dream big. He was so important in my life, as was my mom. Once, when I was angry with my mom and began planning to run away from home, she suggested I wait at least until my dad got home before I left. I didn't think about it then, but her asking me to wait totally took away the point of "running away," but that's what I did. It sounded like a good idea to me because I did want to say good-bye to my dad. So I postponed heading out for the little kudzu-covered shack at the top of the hill where I had planned to make my new home. By the time my dad finally got home I had rethought my position and decided against running away at all. One point for Mom!

Dad loved his job because he loved helping people. He was a good dentist and his staff and patients loved him. Once, when I was about 4 years old, one of the ladies in his office asked me to be a flower girl in her wedding. It was such an honor. I loved wearing the pretty dress and being a part of such an important day. Pictures from that day now remind me of how important my dad was to the people around him. Many people hate their bosses, but not the family of workers who helped my dad conduct his practice.

Dad had a little sign in his one-story office that read "Pain-free dentistry upstairs." I loved Dad's sense of humor and the rock solid stability he gave our family. I am sure he worried about taking care of us, keeping his practice strong, and all the things most adults worry with, but I just never saw that side of him. He seemed to face life with confident optimism.

All of my siblings swam in the very small, very run down pool at the local YMCA. My mom and dad hauled them to practices and swim meets and gave my brother and sisters a lot of encouragement. One day, after a meet, my mom lined up all of my siblings on our front porch for a photograph. Each child held up their swimming ribbons. I stood beside her as she took the photograph and set my heart on winning a ribbon of my own some day.

At age 6, I learned to swim. Mrs. Griffin was our coach at the time and she took on the task to teach me the strokes and all of the basics of swimming. Mrs. Griffin and I also had the same birthday and I always thought that was so cool. Although I was learning how to swim, I wasn't quite old enough to compete, but I tagged along to all the meets just the same. One day, my sister's relay team was a person short. They needed one more "warm" body to be able to compete, so I got the nod. The other swimmers were five years older than I was, but that didn't intimidate me. The other members of my sister's relay team swam first, and I was the last to go. I swam my heart out. I later found out that my mother told someone in the bleachers that she wasn't sure if I was swimming or drowning, but I gave it everything I had. When I finally touched the wall, I looked up, gasping for breath and with all sincerity asked, "Did I win?"

From that moment on, I had the fever. I was shocked to learn that I hadn't won, but I had felt the thrill of competition and after that, I began to train even harder. When I was 8 years old, my dad took me to a meet two hours away in Columbia, SC. I was the scrawny, little kid in the outside lane wearing a baggy stars-and-stripes bathing suit and dreaming of swimming in the Olympics. But there was something special about that particular swim meet as each time I touched the end of the pool, the timer would say, "Honey, that's another state record."

My dad was so proud of his baby girl. He started a tradition after that meet. Before a race, if he saw I was getting anxious, he'd say "Marian, don't get nervous just because this is the most important race of your life." His joking around always helped me calm down and focus on the task at hand.

From that first meet on, I set big goals and went after them with fierce determination. I began swimming in the morning before school, and hit the pool again after school. It was a rigorous schedule, but I loved it. The meets were magical to me. When I stepped up on the start platform, I would try to clear my mind. I'd grab the edge of the block and pull back ready to launch myself through the air and into the water. It is a wonderful thing when you hear the start whistle or horn, when the roars of the crowd disappear as you enter the water. Once you dive in, there is a wonderful calm, even as you pour all that you have into your kick and strokes. When you surface to breathe, the roar returns, but this time all you hear is the noise of the water as you cut a path through it. Swimming has a beautiful rhythm; the cadence of your breath and the pounding of your heart. Sometimes, you are aware of the other swimmers, someone who is ahead of you or gaining on you, but when you are really at your best, there is only you and the water.

My dad saw my love for swimming and was always there for me, as was my mom. When I was 11, Dad got me a bench press for my birthday. Not your typical "girly-girl" birthday present, but I thought it was great. From the outside, others might have thought he was putting too much pressure on me, but it was just his way of supporting my dreams and I appreciated it. He'd say "go for the scholarship," and I heard that as a vote of confidence, not pressure to perform.

Whether or I won or lost, my parents were proud of me and let me know it. Once, I was to swim the butterfly stroke in our State Meet. That's a tough stroke, but it was one of my favorites. I was nervous and young, and as I started, I took one stroke of freestyle. I won the race and even broke a new state record, but I knew in my heart that I couldn't take the win. I clearly should have been disqualified, but the stroke judge obviously hadn't seen it. I suppose I was tempted not to disqualify myself. I did love winning, but I knew from my parent's teachings that integrity is what you do when no one else is looking and I wouldn't have felt right taking the gold under those pretenses. Therefore, I told the judges what I'd done and watched as the other girls took their places on the platform. On the ride home, my parents placed their arms around me and said, "That might have been the most important race of your life, Marian." I had done the right thing and that was more important to my parents than any win. Truth is, I felt good about my decision, as well.

My parents had to be exhausted. We'd go to swim meets in and out of the state, they would sit on hard metal bleachers all weekend, and then they'd return to work the next day after late nights on the road. They did it out of sheer love and true grit. Parents that show their love in actions are a blessing.

When I entered middle school, my mom would drive me over to Clemson University, which was about 30 minutes away, so I could train with the college team. Our swim program was very small and on several occasions there was not even a swim team in Anderson. Regardless, my parents helped me find a way to keep swimming and going for my goals. At Clemson, mom would sit in the bleachers and work on her sewing while I practiced. More than once, I caught her looking at the beautifully built men on the college swim team. When I teased her about it, she looked up from her sewing and said, "Just because you're on a diet doesn't mean you can't look at the menu, Marian."

Sight-seeing benefits aside, my mother had to be relieved when Anderson hired a new swim coach and the city built two 25-meter pools, one on either side of the city. The new pools spurred interest in swimming and we were able to finally draw in some good coaches. Our team, which at one time consisted of just me and only one other swimmer, (Gary Long), grew tremendously and our team actually won the State Championship Title my junior year in high school. This was completely unheard of for our little team, but we did it!

Sometimes, swimming seemed to eat up my entire life. I passed on church ski trips and other outings to avoid the risk of injury, but I worked too hard to give up, and I didn't want to quit. I stuck to it; and in my senior year, I became the first person from my hometown to ever earn a swimming scholarship. You would have thought I had won an Oscar. It was truly the proudest moment of my life!

I looked at colleges as far away as Oklahoma and even took a trip to see the campus. My parents tried to give me freedom as I chose which school I would attend, but after the trip out to Oklahoma, my parent's hearts just weren't in it. They finally said, "You know Marian, you'll never be able to come home for dinner if you go way out there."

Dinner as a family may be a simple thing, but when I was growing up, we loved that time together. We looked forward to when Dad came home after work. Even after a full day at the office, he had time, energy, and love for us and mom always had something good to eat. To this little college-bound home-body, the thought of coming home for dinner now and then sounded like a good thing. So I joyfully accepted a scholarship offer from Clemson.

Chapter 6 Healing waters

"It's not a book. It's a weapon. A weapon aimed right at the hearts and minds of the weak and the desperate. It will give us control of them. If we want to rule more than one small town, we have to have it. People will come from all over, they'll do exactly what I tell 'em if the words are from the book. It's happened before and it'll happen again. All we need is that book."

-Carnegie, in The Book of Eli

In the movie "The Book of Eli," Denzel Washington plays the hero in a post-nuclear war drama. He was led by a voice to the only remaining copy of the Bible and told to protect the book, read it, and "take it West." The movie is full of violence and cannibalism in a world where water is scare and human compassion is almost non-existent. The land is dry and dying just like the souls of the people. Eli comes to know the power of the book, of living water, as it changes him to make him stronger and more grateful, and it expands his ability to love. The villain of the movie is a man who also knows the power of the book Eli carries. He wants the Bible so that he can use it to control people.

When my husband and I were dating, he would quote Bible verses. He impressed me with his knowledge, and I always felt so inferior to him where the Bible was concerned. He said people had always told him that he was going to make a preacher some day. As our marriage deteriorated, if I tried to tell him that I thought he should treat me differently, he would quote scripture and use "God talk." Sometimes, the verses he used from the Bible made me feel that as his wife, I was his property. It was as if he had God's seal on whatever he wanted to do with me: good or bad. It was almost enough to make me give up on God, except for this gentle comfort in my soul and the kindness of a handful of God's children.

Church was one place the kids and I were "allowed" to go. His mother and father would take us to the small Baptist church just up the road. I was so grateful for the opportunity to ride in a car, to get out of the house, to be around people, to talk and laugh. And yes, to forget the pain at home. The kids sang in the children's choir and I loved to watch them as they sang. I know pride is a sin, but I'm confessing: I was proud! They opened up when they sang, particularly Sydney. She sang with her entire body and seemed to completely lose herself in the songs. I was not raised Baptist, so I didn't know all of the practices of that denomination, but I knew kindness when I experienced it and that was enough to make me feel a part of this family of believers.

Like every church I've ever visited or been a part of, its members were imperfect. I liked that about them. Some of the people who sat in the pews beside me were very open about their shortcomings, some of them were self-righteous. All of them were searching, just like I was. I didn't know what they were dealing with when they went home, just like they didn't know about my private hell. But we treated each other with respect. I needed the comfort they offered me and felt myself gain strength with every kind word of encouragement they gave me or my children.

Once, the choir director sent home a CD for the children to practice with for the week. They were wide-eyed and excited as they put the disc into the little boom box. Like many other nights, my husband came home drunk, but the children couldn't wait to show him what they had gotten at church. In anger and for no good reason, he grabbed the disc out of the player and proceeded to use his pocket knife to scratch the entire CD. On another occasion, he saw where I had marked in my Bible so I could simply find a passage more quickly. He went into a tirade, tore the Bible from my hands and threw it into the flaming hot wood stove. Both occasions destroyed the children and left me bewildered and searching for any way to understand what motivated him. I would cry out to God like the psalmist in the angry verses in the Psalms. I know that Jesus wants us to pray for our enemies, so I prayed that God would strike him dead. That might not have been what Jesus meant, but I didn't want to lie to God when I prayed. What I really wanted in those moments was for God to send my husband to a fire hotter than the flames in the wood stove where my Bible was now nothing but ash. That sounds wrong, but that's what I felt, and I trusted God to be able to handle my fury.

After his worst days, however, my husband would rebound quickly. He said all the right things and made a lot of promises. That's what people who are sick do. He would beg for forgiveness and promise to be a better husband, stop drinking, and come home in time for us to have dinner as a family. He would talk about when we got the "big settlement" from the wreck some day. He promised to get me another car to drive so I could go to the grocery store or doctor like most moms. When he was kind to me, I was hearing exactly what I needed to hear, so I continued to stay with him. I so desperately wanted him to love me and to be worth changing for. I found I could live for weeks and months on the few "crumbs" he handed to me.

One Sunday in church, Mama Dot mentioned to me that there would be a baptism the next Sunday. Deep in my heart, I knew that it was time for me to be baptized. This church was my family and I wanted to become an official member. I still did not claim to know all that I needed to know about the Bible or about being a Baptist, but I knew with all of my heart that I wanted to be a part of this church. I wanted to commit my heart, soul, and efforts as a member of this congregation. Of course, I couldn't make a decision like that without talking to my husband first, so I asked him about it later that day. Initially, he said he was fine with the idea. I then walked up to my in-law's house and called the pastor to ask that he add my name to the list of those who would be baptized the next Sunday.

The pastor was almost as excited as I was. He and his wife had become very dear to me in the years that we lived in the little concrete house. When my husband had refused to allow me to see a doctor while I was pregnant with our third child, the pastor's wife, who was a doula, or midwife of sorts, confronted him. She told my husband that if he didn't take me to the doctor immediately, the Department of Social Services would be in the hospital room when the baby was born and he would have many difficult questions to answer. Her words motivated him to finally allow me to begin my prenatal care, but by that time, I was 30 weeks pregnant. It had also been a more difficult pregnancy for me for a few reasons. For one thing, I was much older and had been weakened by the car wreck. In addition, I had been cruelly mistreated for years. On one occasion when I complained of being nauseous, my husband "helped me" by brutally jamming his fingers deep down my throat to make me vomit. I was extremely concerned about the baby and this particular pregnancy and was so grateful that my pastor's wife had been so courageous.

I had been tormented early in the pregnancy with my own feelings of guilt. It wasn't that I didn't want another child. It was that I didn't want another child with "this" man. I was forbidden by my husband to use contraceptives of any kind, and he would joke about what good babies he made. It was crude, but he wasn't wrong. Our children are all beautiful, but more importantly, they are each extremely kind-hearted, and loving. I often wondered if God had been especially generous to my three knowing what lay ahead?

After my precious Dorothy (who we affectionately called "Dodie" the first few years of her life) was born, the people of my church were almost as excited as Sydney and Hunter. The way they loved all of us was a beautiful expression of what church should be.

When I called the pastor to tell him that I wanted to be baptized, he prayed for me and told me to come early to church the next Sunday. By Wednesday night, however, my husband had changed his mind about my baptism. He couldn't articulate why he did not want me to be baptized, he just told me I wouldn't be allowed to go through with it. Over and over, he said I wasn't doing it for the right reasons. I asked him what he thought my reasons were, but he never gave me an answer. He just began making horrible threats. He told me that the scar on his forehead was proof that he belonged to a "special group" who would do whatever he said, so I could never get away from him. Sometimes, his threats terrified me, but other times I could see them as dribble. He was in the driver's seat, though, and he knew precisely how to control me.

In the days that followed, he changed his mind again and decided I could be baptized. By this time I was an emotional mess. This was supposed to be a special time for me. It was supposed to be about God, about death and resurrection, about renewed hope, about being made clean, about new life. I tried so hard not to let him take that from me, but the week became a roller coaster of "You can. You can't." By Saturday night, it came to violent blows. After much yelling and screaming on his part and batting me around, he ultimately tried to push my head through the glass-paned door on our front porch. Somehow I got away from him and locked myself in the bedroom. He stormed around trying to get to me, but eventually, he passed out on the couch as was his habit.

The next morning, I got up and dressed the children just like every other Sunday. My in-laws came early to drive us to church. They knew nothing of the beating from the night before and I didn't tell them. Mama Dot told her son when the service would start and encouraged him not to be late. We closed the door and headed for church.

At the little church, everyone was abuzz with preparations for the baptisms. Those of us who were to be baptized were shown where we would wait and told of the plans for the service. It was the strangest thing: my body and my heart were bruised by that man, but I still hoped he would be there. I had a somber moment before we were baptized when I was able to sit and pray quietly. I was off to myself and I wept. My body hurt and I felt so unworthy of anyone's love, let alone God's love. I know this makes me sound like I'm crazy, but at my weakest moment, I felt arms around me as I sat in the corner of that room behind the altar.

When I opened my eyes and wiped the tears away, no one was there, but I still felt the warm, strong arms around me. In an instant, all fear left me and I was confident that I was doing the right thing...and for the right reasons.

As we walked into the water, I looked out across the faces in the church. My in-laws, my children, my friends were all there, but I could not find my husband among the faces. For a split second I wondered if I should not go through with the baptism. By stepping back now, though, I felt as though my secrets would be well noticed. So I walked up to the pastor with the water just to my waist. He smiled at me and said words that have been spoken above flowing rivers around the world, words that have echoed in cathedrals and small churches for thousands of years. He talked about "unmerited favor," a love I could not be pretty enough, sweet enough, or smart enough to earn. He talked about love that I could not be ugly enough, mean enough, or foolish enough to lose. I closed my eyes as he eased my body beneath the water. Water is home to this swimmer. My feet began to float up and I pressed them down toward the bottom of the pool. I tried not to worry about what my husband was going to do to me because I had disobeyed him. I tried to hear what the preacher was saying. I tried to believe that what he was saying was true, and I prayed that God was really washing me clean, that I was really being buried and resurrected, and that I was going to get a new life.

When my husband began yelling at me that night because he had arrived at the church too late to see me baptized, I felt that promised, renewed strength and began to formulate a way to take my children and run.

Chapter 7 Remembrance

You can hide 'neath your covers and study your pain
Make crosses from your lovers, throw roses in the rain
Waste your summer praying in vain
for a savior to rise from these streets.

Bruce Springsteen, Thunder Roads

When things were particularly bad with my husband, I would allow myself some self-pity and inflate how wonderful things probably were with my friends and family. It's easy to feel alone and forgotten when you live with someone who works to make you feel that way.

To keep myself grounded after I had spent hours listening to the ravings of a man who was drunk out of his mind, I would lie in my bed and inventory all the good people I had known in my life. Some people, like my mom and dad, stood out. Gary Long, one of my swim teammates, was also always a fond memory.

We affectionately referred to Gary as "Gooey" because he had a fondness for the gooey-est desserts before and at a swim meet. He said they gave him energy and to see him swim, I began to believe he was right. His parents and mine would continually take turns driving us to the meets. After I started driving, we'd have heated arguments when he'd want to sleep in and risk making me late for practice. I'd lay on the horn until he was in the car and then I'd lay on a lecture for the ride. I'd fuss, he'd roll his eyes at me, he and I would somehow get through practice, and then inevitably, we'd always ride home as best buddies. He truly was my "brother from another mother."

Gary's dad, Dr. Needham Long, was a pathologist. I was always cracking jokes about his name: "Where's Neeham when you <u>need</u> <u>him</u>?" Gary's mom, Miss Winnie, was tender and nurturing to Gary and to me. Gary is a doctor now. He and his precious wife, Kim, have three wonderful children. I would remember the Longs when the madness of my world made me forget who I used to be.

Memories of my college swim mates also helped me hold onto a confidence in humanity. When I first began swimming at Clemson, I was afraid we'd never really mesh as a team. Except for our love of swimming, we seemed to have very little in common. My teammates were from all over the country, and each of us had been celebrities of sorts in our hometowns. We were all accustomed to seeing our name in headlines for front page news stories and being treated like heroes. At Clemson we were surrounded by exceptional athletes, and we had to remold our egos to learn how and where we fit in and to become a unified team.

It was 1982 when I began at Clemson, and some of the girls kept talking about "The Boss." My high school years had been pretty much nothing but swimming. I had no idea who all the screaming and giggling was about until they introduced me to Bruce Springsteen. His music became important to me, just as it is too much of my generation. We'd belt out his deep and meaningful anthems *Jungleland* and *Thunder Roads* as if they were doo-wop sing-alongs. We really hadn't lived enough to understand the deep meaning in his lyrics. Maybe our souls got it: the longing to escape that pounded in the baseline of most of the songs on the *Born to Run* album. But in our naive youth, we were too distracted by Bruce's cute behind clad in Levis to really pay attention to the words he was singing. We'd stay up late gossiping, giggling and dreaming. We even started a silly little way to say our names: Robin was Ra-hobin; Terry was Ta-herry, Judy was Ja-hoodie, Jannie was Ja-hanney, and my name was Ma-hairian. I don't know if it was their way of making fun of how many syllables this Southern girl added to words or not; but whatever the reason, the names stuck.

I swam my all-time best my freshman year thanks to some very hard work and the way the older teammates took me in and showed me the ropes. After the Senior Nationals, I slowed my training a bit and I gained some weight. A coach made a comment about my size, and my reaction was an over-reaction. I increased my training in the pool and wasn't eating enough to fuel my body. I dropped from 138 lean pounds to 128 pounds. I was on the verge of a breakdown and didn't even realize it. I was so proud to have dropped the weight and was unable to see the immense harm I was doing to my body.

It was then that my mom drove up to Clemson with a purpose... and props. She pulled out a candle and lit it on both ends. Just in case I was missing her point, she held a flame to the middle of the candle. I looked past the fire and wax between me and my mother and saw the loving concern in her eyes. Mom is a strong woman who deeply loves all of her children. With her support and the help of my teammates, I began to eat regularly again. Unfortunately, I had weakened my body to the point that I was unable to live up to what I knew had been my potential. I was disappointed in myself, but I didn't sense that from any of my friends. They had my back and had been truly worried about me. I didn't know it then, but they would order pizzas even when they weren't hungry just to get me to eat. I'll never forget the love they showed me. They were all just glad to see me on the mend.

I guess on some level as I lay in my bed after my husband had belittled, bruised, and battered me, I was waiting for one of those good friends to rescue me. I didn't know they were all praying for me, cheering for me, and waiting for me to take the first step. What I've learned is that people in abusive situations say they want help, but when it comes, they shy away from it because the abuse is what they know. The abnormality of abuse begins to seem normal and it's so hard to let go. You'd think it would be an easy decision to leave someone who was continually abusing you. I agonized over when to leave, how to leave, and I worried about the life my children would lead if I stayed or if I left. My life was a continual cycle of madness. I waited. I wondered. I prayed about what to do next.

Chapter 8 Summer adventures

South Carolina is a beautiful state. It is green and lush. My hometown is on the western side of the state near the blue waters of Lake Hartwell which forms part of the border between South Carolina and Georgia. The coastal part of the state is the image of the Deep South with old oaks draped with Spanish Moss. The Angel Oak near Charleston is said to be the oldest living thing east of the Mississippi. Its roots run deep because the tree has been nourished by the rich soil for hundreds of years. Its massive, swooping branches have grown so large and heavy that the tree cannot hold her own limbs. Man-made large beams support the larger branches like a walker steadies a fragile old woman. Growing up, I never felt a desperate need to escape my home except for that one "run-away" flop. Some of my friends seem to be filled with an impetuous restlessness, like they had to get away. I wanted big things, and I knew I would have to uproot to have them, but if I was running it would be toward something not away from my home.

Summer breaks during my college years afforded me opportunities to see parts of the country that were very different from South Carolina. After my freshman year, my roommate, Ja-hoodie, and I were counselors at the world-renowned Texas Longhorn Swim Camp. Texas is every bit as hot and humid as South Carolina, but it was definitely wider and more open. It was the perfect place for Ja-hoodie and me to spread our wings a little. At the Longhorn Camp we rubbed shoulders with some very well-known coaches like Chris Kirschner and US Olympic Coaches Richard Quick and Eddie Reese. These men were giants in the swimming world and we felt completely surrounded by success.

We and the other camp counselors watched over 600 swimmers over a 6 week period. We helped them in the pool and were in charge of their dry land training, as well. We had access to the weight room and the football field used by the Texas Longhorns. We thought we were so mature and on top of the world.

The following summer, I joined my high school teammate Gary Long and a former coach in Albuquerque, New Mexico to train for the summer. I roomed with one of my former teammates, Shannon. Gooey and his roommate from Auburn shared an apartment with us near the University of New Mexico. We trained early in the morning and again in the afternoon. To earn some extra cash, we each took on summer jobs. I was appointed Head Coach for the Coronado Air Force Base Swim Team. I'm still not sure how I landed that job, but I had kids of all ages on my team, ranging from "I can't make it to the end of the pool" to some exceptional athletes. My coach, Dave, loaned me his little pea green car to drive around Albuquerque, but I usually stuck with a bike that had been loaned to me by one of the local swimmers. I would use it during the day as I could move in and out of traffic much easier and it gave me that much more of an edge over my competitors. In the evenings, we would pile into the little pea green car and take a road trip to watch the sunset. It was a relaxing way to wind down after a busy day. Sometimes there are moments when even an over-the-top college kid who thinks she's got the world by the tail has to be silent. One weekend we drove to Carlsbad Cavern to watch the bats take to the night sky. They look like wisps of black smoke as they fly from the cavern every evening to hunt and explore. They return home each morning before daylight to the safety of the cavern. It's easier to venture out when you know you can return home. It's easier to leave when you know what you're looking for.

Chapter 9 End of a dream

When my first marriage had ended, I was surprised to find that I was depressed and sad that I had not been able to make my marriage work. I viewed the end of my marriage as a horrible personal failure. It was hard to keep my mind focused due to the shame I felt for getting a divorce. It was supposed to have been a forever thing, and I was really hurt that it turned out the way it did. I was not angry at my former husband. He and I had met my senior year at Clemson. He was a good man and I know I loved him, but we both had decided it was for the best. Divorce is so common that you think, "it must not be that bad." Then you experience it and you know the unbearable pain of ending something you had hoped would last forever.

Mom and Dad had since moved from my childhood home by that time and offered to let me stay in the house I had grown up in for a while. As we moved boxes from the car into the empty house, my dad, who had a way of leaving smiles behind him like footprints, tried to comfort me. We laughed a lot - probably too much under the circumstances- but that was Dad's way. Dad always wanted to keep me focused on the bright side of things. I could tell he didn't want to leave me in my thoughts; but eventually, he climbed in his car, waved goodbye, and left me to pull newspaper-wrapped cups and glasses from the boxes and get comfortable with being by myself. I was very lonely and very vulnerable, but I could not have named those feelings then.

As luck would have it, just after I moved back into the house I had grown up in it sold. It was then that I had to go out and get my first "big girl" apartment, which was probably much better for me in the long run.

Soon after that, my dad found out he had colon cancer. I remember driving to Charleston to be with my mom and dad the day of his first surgery. I arrived to see him smiling and joking with the nursing staff. I sat in the chair beside his bed and listened as he answered the nurse's questions. When she asked him if he was allergic to anything, I thought in my head, he's going to say something like "ugly women," I just know it. Well, no sooner had that thought crossed my mind, when my dad stated just that, simply and matter of fact, "ugly women." The nurse, who happened to be adorable, looked a little startled at first and then she realized he was joking. It was then that I totally lost it and not just because Dad had said it, but because I had absolutely expected him to.

Knowing the seriousness of what my dad was facing made the levity even funnier. The next day, when the nurse came in to roll Dad down to surgery, it was as if someone in the casting department for a movie had heard Dad's earlier joke. I am certain the nurse was a kind, loving professional; but when we saw her, it was all we could do not to start laughing again. As cruel as this will sound, and I would never hurt anyone's feeling like this, but there is no other way to say it... there stood the ugliest nurse any of us had ever seen. But the great thing was we all saw her as a gift from God, even Dad. As worried as we were, we couldn't help but chuckle as dad disappeared down the hallway, escorted by the "angelic" nurse, on his way to surgery.

We would retell that story, as gently as we could, as family members and friends checked on Dad and we waited on the surgeon's updates. Our laughing quieted, however, when the news from the surgeon was not good. The cancer had spread through the walls of Dad's colon and they would have to perform a full colostomy in the next few weeks.

Dad lived the rest of his life with a colostomy bag attached to a port in his side. The bag slowed him down some, but it certainly did not stop him. He regained a lot of his strength and was even able to play tennis again. He would later tell me, as he was on his death bed at home, that he'd give anything to go out and feel the sun on his face, and the sweat on his skin, to just get in one more set of tennis. He was a wonderful man who loved the simple things in life and he knew the splendor of each day.

In November 1997, the same year as my car wreck, my mother called each of the children to let us know we needed to say our goodbyes to Dad.

I do not have many complimentary words about my second husband, my children's father, but he agreed to take care of the children while I went to be with my dad. It was a kindness I had not expected from him, but one, which even today, I still appreciate. I consider it such a blessing that I was able to reminisce with my father in those last days of his life. Dad was in severe pain, but he kept his wits about him. It was as if he were giving us the best of him as he knew his days were numbered. In fact, every day we had with him in those last days had a purpose. Very close by was a means to end his life, but despite the pain he endured, he was steadfast, and his faith saw him through to the very end. I have often wondered what I would have done in the same situation. Would I have been able to handle all the pain and suffering with the same dignity and strength he showed? I so hope I would have.

In those precious last new moments we had together, my dad and I talked about swim meets and all the fun times we had shared. We talked about the close races which he said made his heart pound out of his chest as they watched me race to the wall. I cried and looked in his eyes and told him things I had told him hundreds of times: "I love you. I am honored to be your child. I am stronger because I have known you." My dad always knew those things, but I guess I just needed to say them again.

As Thanksgiving approached, we had to leave the house we were staying in to allow the family to return for the holiday, so I said goodbye to my dad the day before Thanksgiving. A part of me knew this would be the last time I would ever talk to my dad, face to face, that is. My plan had been to go back to care for my children and then return in a few days. The hope of that plan was the only way that I was able to walk out of the room and leave my father that day. But it was a gentle comfort that was not to be. On the Sunday after Thanksgiving, my father lost his battle with cancer, but he entered into Heavens gates.

As painful as losing Dad was, I was still grateful. I was grateful that he had an opportunity to say goodbye to friends and family and had been surrounded by such love in his last days. He faced his death with confidence in God's miraculous grace and mercy, which was a comfort to all of us. I was grateful that he was no longer suffering. Most of all, I was grateful for the privilege of having such a wonderful father.

Getting through the funeral wasn't easy for any of us, especially my mom, but God delivered on His promise for strength and comfort. Dad's service was held in Beaufort, a five-hour trek from the town where he had lived most of his life and built his dental practice, yet many wonderful friends made the drive to say their last goodbyes to a much-loved man.

Dad had asked that he be cremated, so at the funeral and afterwards at the funeral home, Dad's friends would carry his ashes around in a beautiful wooden box. It was as if they were taking him around to enjoy the party. We'd joke about who "had" my dad. He would have loved it, though, as he so liked to get together with friends and family. He always was the "life" of the party and even in death, he still was on that day of days.

In the weeks that followed my Dad's death, I began journaling to get my thoughts and feelings on paper. I've taken the liberty to print the pages of a tribute I wrote for my father:

BLESSED IS A MAN

Blessed is a man
Who grows up in a quaint little town and though he doesn't know it at the time, builds friendships that will last his lifetime.
Blessed is a man
Who goes to fight for his country in seas a world away and lives to come home and tell about it.
Blessed is a man
Who, though quite shy, finds the courage to ask the tall woman he spies across the dance floor for a dance. The woman, in fact, who would become his wife, his soul mate, the mother of his children, and the woman he would love the rest of his life.
Blessed is a man
Who has the knowledge, determination, and persistence to build a successful dental practice. One who is held in the highest regard by others in his field and community, and is always willing to help out a newcomer.
Blessed is a man
Who willingly shares his precious time with each of his four children, cheering each of them on in their successes and picking them up in their failures always being approachable to talk to and showing unconditional love in its truest form.
Blessed is a man
Who has health, wealth, and happiness, and never lets it get the best of him, always remaining humble and generous to all.
Blessed is a man

Who, over the years, gains so many friends, possibly too many to count, but never too many to love.
Blessed is a man
Who is able to see all of his grandchildren born into this world and for them to feel and share his love.*
Blessed is a man
Who, when afflicted with a deadly disease, learns to fight it with every bone in his body, and is brave enough to meet it head on; maintaining his dignity at all times, and never losing his unique sense of humor.

Blessed is a man
Who is given the most precious gift of time
Time to ask forgiveness of his sins
Time to befriend his foes
Time to reflect on his life and look forward to the eternal life
Time to prepare his loved ones for his physical absence by leaving no stone unturned, no question unanswered.
Blessed is a man
Who can see his family unite at his side once more and say his last good-byes to each of them.
Blessed is a man
Who puts his total faith in the Lord and accepts His wondrous gift of grace.
Blessed is a man
Who leaves this world in the comfort of his home, in the loving arms of his wife, to be immediately cradled by the loving arms of Jesus, as he enters the Almighty Kingdom of Heaven.
Blessed is a man
Who lived such a full and wondrous life, and who knew the splendor of each day.
Truly blessed are we to have been a part of his life here on earth. We loved him and were loved by him.
He was a Son
He was a Brother
He was a Husband
He was a Father
He was a Friend
He was

MARIAN WARDLAW

Samuel Earle Wardlaw
and
he was blessed
I love you Dad

*(Needless to say, this was written before we knew of Dorothy. He would have so loved her, as well as Sydney, Hunter and his other grandchildren.)

Chapter 10 Silver bells

He had smoked since he was 14 years old, so we should not have been surprised when my father-in-law, Papa Bill, was diagnosed with lung cancer. The doctors were blunt: it would kill him. It was just a question of when. Sydney drew closer to her grandfather even though his treatment and weakness from the illness meant they had less time together. She did not want to lose him, and together we struggled with the questions that everyone has when someone they love is dying.

One Saturday morning, Mama Dot had rushed Papa Bill to the hospital because of complications of his lung cancer. We, however, got a surprise knock on the door, and as usual, my husband forbade us to answer. He routinely would make us go into the back of the house and would do whatever it took to keep us from opening the door. This morning, I must have eaten my Wheaties because I stood up to him and told him he needed to answer the door or I would. To my surprise, he did; and standing on the front porch was a police officer.

I had never been so happy to see the police in all my life! I was saddened that my children had to see their father arrested, but I was so grateful that someone had called him on his illegal behavior. "Finally," I said to myself, "finally!"

As the police left my driveway with my husband locked in the back of the car, I looked over at his truck. It had been exactly five years since the automobile accident that left me without a car. I hadn't driven since March 1997 and it was now March 2002. And there, right in front of me was a truck... and my husband was in custody so he couldn't hurt me if I used it. On one hand, it would be a perfect time to run; on the other, I knew the terrible trauma that Bill and Dot were going through.

I piled all three children into the truck and shuttered to shake off all of the emotion I was feeling. I put the key in the ignition, started the engine and pulled the gearshift into drive. Driving gives you such a feeling of control. You press the accelerator and you move forward, you turn the wheel and completely change your direction and your destiny. I turned the truck toward Anderson, to the hospital where our beloved Papa Bill was fighting for his life.

When I reached the hospital, I asked family members to watch the children while I talked with Bill and Dot. In private, I told them what had happened with their son. As I broke the news to them, you could see the disappointment in each of their eyes. It crushed me to have to tell them, but I knew they needed to know. I explained that their son had taken money from customers for electrical jobs and failed to do the work. My husband's brothers were also in the room and they all agreed that the best course of action would be to let him stay in jail rather than bail him out instantly. I was so glad they all made that decision. I had no access to money if he needed to post bail, but they did and could have helped him dodge the consequences of his behavior once again. I told them again how sorry I was to have to bring such bad news to them, then I gathered my children and returned home. Little did I know, but that was the most peaceful night I had experienced in many, many years. I could even sense a peaceful calm in the children, as well, especially Sydney. She was getting old enough to know that something wasn't right with her dad, and I could feel how relieved she was. That night, there was no ranting and raving. There was no screaming, no hitting. That night we had some long awaited peace and quiet. Such a long-awaited, yet welcomed visitor, indeed.

In the weeks that followed, I began to get some faith in the justice system. Fear that the courts would allow my husband to have custody of my children had been one of the main reasons I did not leave. I heard horror stories about abusive parents getting custody. I had not worked outside the home in more than five years and was afraid the courts would doubt my ability to provide for my children. I know I had my doubts. But with my husband in jail, I was emboldened. I knew he would be out soon, but the fact that he had finally been arrested had given me new hope.

When Papa Bill died, my husband was on his best behavior and played the role of a loving son. It sickened me because he had shown such disrespect to his father for so many years. I wasn't the only one it upset. Just weeks earlier, members of his own family had almost called the police on him, but he stood there in front of all of them and acted like an angel. I am certain he thought he loved his father, but love shows itself in actions, and my husband's actions toward his father were selfish, cruel, and downright disrespectful.

Papa Bill was such a meticulous man, but because of his illness he had been unable to care for his yard or ours. Before he got so sick, though, he would come up to our yard and let Hunter ride on his big red tractor with him as he cut the grass. They both enjoyed that so much and Hunter looked forward to those special times with Papa Bill with great anticipation. Knowing of Papa Bill's love for a well-kept yard, I asked my husband to please mow our yard and his parents' yard before the funeral. He assured me he would, but when Papa Bill made his last ride by our little, concrete house, albeit in the hearse, the grass was overgrown and unkempt. I wish I could have found a way to mow it myself in honor of this sweet, precious man who had cared for our yard and us so many times. It just broke my heart and I was embarrassed at my husband's final lack of decency.

On the bright side, when I remember Papa Bill, I remember him best with Sydney in his arms. At the funeral home, Sydney slowly walked up to his body in the casket. I watched her closely to make sure she was okay as she said goodbye to her precious Papa Bill. When I turned away for a brief second, she pulled a coin from her pocket that someone had just given her in the receiving line. She then proceeded to, ever so gently, place the shiny, silver coin smack dab on his forehead and smiled. That might have seemed irreverent to some, but Papa Bill and Sydney had a secret love language. For most of her life, he'd bring her tiny chocolate kisses which she called "silver bells." Sydney didn't have a "silver bell" that day, so a silver coin would have to do.

Chapter 11 Your trash, my treasure

"I merely took the energy it takes to pout and wrote some blues."
Duke Ellington

To cope during the worst days in the concrete house, I didn't do a lot of deep soul searching. I knew that someday I'd have to rummage around in the dusty attic of my psyche if I was ever to heal and understand why I had attracted and stayed married to an abuser. It might have saved me some suffering down the road if I had stopped and done the work earlier. But I didn't think I would survive if I tore myself down while I lived with a man who made that his life's work. So instead, I focused on my blessings. Every day, I made a point of looking for the brief moments of beauty that moved me toward the strength I needed. Usually, those moments came through my children.

I also discovered during the darkest days of my life that making things strengthened me. Maybe it's because our Maker is creative, so we are more like him when we put our heart and soul into creating something good. As early as Sydney's first birthday, I discovered a love for baking unique birthday cakes. My mother-in-law would drive me to Walmart to choose icings and look for ideas. The night before a birthday, I'd stay up until after my husband had passed out and work for hours to get everything just right. Over the years, I made every kind of cake, from Tweety Bird to a pretty pink princess. With no money, I had to make use of what I found around me, so I used my imagination and turned pecans from our yard into the heads of the characters. Sydney's all-time favorite was a Sleeping Beauty cake, complete with fairies and mean ol' Maluficent. The cake was complete with a handsome prince to rescue the beautiful, sleeping beauty.

Hunter's cakes ranged from Teenage Ninja Turtles to a Spiderman cake. Boys want to be heroes, even if they are mutant reptiles named for 15th Century artists. By the time Dorothy came along, we had fled to Georgia, but the cakes remained an important tradition for our family, so I continued the late nights to create lady bug cakes with Twizzlers for legs or any creation I could come up with that I knew would make my children smile.

At Christmas, I'd create angels from Pringles cans. It was symbolic to me: taking what someone else would see as trash and making something valuable and worthwhile. With a Christmas bulb for a head and tissue paper for a ball gown, these angels or Santa and Mrs. Claus "angels" were a gift from my heart to my family and friends. The angels were always warmly received. Sydney and Hunter learned at a young age that they could give caring gifts even if they had no money to spend and the time spent would far outweigh a store bought gift. I was thankful they learned that lesson so early and still honor that lesson even today.

I also enlisted the help of an Aunt to learn to crochet. I wanted to make Sydney a hat for her birthday like she had seen on TV. So I went to Aunt Sue's house and came home with my stroller full of books, needles, and yarn. After a few false starts, I finally got the hang of it and made her a hat that was adorable, just like Sydney. Well, almost as adorable. My all-time specialty has been and probably will always be scarves. They can be quite monotonous to make, but I find that it keeps me still and I love the repetition and the straight lines that the yarn makes. I have always found it to be so soothing and I love to give them as gifts.

I also learned to make relatively attractive outfits from hand-me-downs from a 60+ year old aunt. Sounds impossible, but you use what you have.

The last New Year's Eve we spent in the little concrete house, Sydney, Hunter and I took construction paper and markers and made New Year's Eve hats. I gathered all three children in the bedroom while their dad stared at the inside of his eyelids on the couch. We took a photograph that night to record our works of art and to commemorate the beginning of the New Year. When I look at that photograph today, I see how run-down I had become. I look tired, but I remember the hope I had for a better life. I just couldn't give up. And somewhere deep down inside my soul, I could feel it was going to be a very big year.

Chapter 12 Sue and Beth

After I'd graduated from Clemson back in 1986, I had a tough time finding work. I went so far as to make an appointment with the President of Clemson, who was gracious enough to see me, and ask his help in getting me a position. I had learned at an early age if you need or want something done, then by all means, go to the top. So that's what I did. He sent me to see this person and that person and I followed every lead, but as the weeks went by I received no offers. It was then that I met a National Sales Rep with Mary Kay Cosmetics and I joined the Mary Kay team. I was reluctant, at first, to try my hand at Mary Kay; but as I learned about the product and philosophy, I was surprised how much I enjoyed my clients and the consultants I recruited. In less than a year's time, I was a Mary Kay Director and had won the privilege of driving a free, burgundy Grand Am.

Whatever your opinion of a Mary Kay representative, the experience was very rewarding for me. At the annual seminars, I listened to speakers who had built their businesses to extraordinary levels. I would leave pumped up and ready to help everyone I met either become a consultant or a loyal customer.

There was only one problem: I was terrified by the mere thought of asking anyone to do anything that might benefit me. I would say it was shyness, but that word implies that I am afraid to make eye contact or speak out in public. The thought of myself as shy almost makes me laugh hysterically. It's not that I am afraid to talk to anyone. It's just tough for me to ask someone to do something to help me. The strangest thing about it is I know and really believe in Mary Kay products and their business model. It was crazy. I just never wanted to be perceived as pushy and couldn't stand to think that friends might avoid me because they thought I was trying to sell them something. To cope with my fears, I tried to be helpful, respectful and treat people the way I wanted to be treated and prayed that would be enough. I had a small group of consultants and we were very successful for such a small group. Mary Kay gave me confidence and an income, but most importantly, it gave me a loyal group of friends who are still priceless to me. When I started in Mary Kay, I thought I would have preferred a "regular" job, but I could never have known how important the people like Jessie and Jonny would be to me in the most critical moments of my life. They trained me, taught me the ropes, and most importantly, they believed in me. I'll always love them for their faith in me and their love for me.

I continued to sell Mary Kay up until the car accident in 1997 when I could no longer delivery product to my clients. Until then, whenever Mary Kay had a training session in Atlanta, I'd bum a ride with "Sue and Beth." Both women are several years older than I am, and we all were Mary Kay Sales Directors when we met. On those runs to Atlanta, they'd share their samples and ideas for growing my business. My life was so different from that of Sue and Beth. My furnishings in the concrete house were a collection of odds and ends which my husband would occasionally pawn when he needed money. Beth's home was, and still is, always spotless and every fabric and finish in her home blends together beautifully. My clothes were matronly hand-me-downs. Beth dressed meticulously. My marriage filled me with fear. Sue and Beth's husbands were completely devoted to them. Both were so gentle, patient, and kind. At every Clemson home game and most away games, too, Sue, Beth, and their husbands, Kevin and Michael, respectively, were clad in bright orange, tailgating and cheering on the Tigers. I tease Sue and Beth all the time that their blood "runneth" orange as I don't think Clemson would be here today without those two devoted Tiger fans.

I actually met Sue's husband, Kevin, in an aerobics class some three years before I actually started my Mary Kay business. The two of them love to travel and make regular trips to Las Vegas and Biloxi and spend time with their grandkids and parents. Sue's husband loves flying a simulator program on his computer and is fascinated with airplanes. On pretty days, you could just about bet Sue's husband was on top of his carport spotting planes. Sue and her husband, Kevin, bowled every Thursday night and would frequently see my husband at the alley, playing Keno with our family's money for hours on end.

Just about everyone can remember where they were when the O.J.

Simpson verdict was announced. Sue, Beth and I were all glued to the television at Beth's house when the gavel came crashing down. Both Sue and Beth knew that my husband was abusive; but even through the O.J. trial they never pressured me for answers to their most sought after questions. With gentle encouragement and sacrificial generosity, they just let me know they would be there when I was ready. Once, as the television reporters played the 911 calls that Nicole Simpson had made during her marriage to O.J., it took everything I had to keep myself together. I didn't blink an eye as I focused on the screen and pretended I didn't feel their eyes on me.

Sue, Beth, and their precious husbands were at the hospital when Hunter was born. Kevin even filmed most of the day's events until I told him to turn off the recorder just before Hunter came barreling into this world, fast and furious. They had been at a Clemson basketball game when Sydney had come into this world. They all love her like crazy, but the sure thing of a Clemson game had trumped the chance that I might deliver that weekend. When Sydney was born, they made an announcement over the intercom to let everyone know about the newest little Clemson Tiger. We still laugh about that when they call to wish Sydney a happy birthday. After Dodie was born, I called my mom and dad and then immediately dialed Sue and Beth's numbers. Mary Kay had expanded my family and given me two lifelong friends who were as strong and courageous as they were kind. To me and my children, they are and forever will be family.

Chapter 13 Enough

In the months that followed Papa Bill's funeral, the courts required my husband to make restitution to the people he had defrauded. If he could not come up with the money, he'd be returned to jail, so he turned to his grieving mother. I felt the tension in his mother's home as he went to talk to her about the money he needed. His mother routinely bailed him out of all of his messes, and I knew she would again; but in her emotional state, so soon since she had lost Papa Bill, she was exactly where I always was: there was no way she could do what she considered the right thing and avoid his swelling rage. I remember Hunter came running in to the den and I quickly asked a family member to take the children outside to play.

How Mama Dot was so calm was beyond me. He was taking advantage of her kindness at every turn; and because she was helping him, he was angry. Of course, it is one thing to take abuse for yourself and quite another to stand by and watch someone else be abused. I started to defend my mother-in-law. He screamed "You, shut up!" It was on that day I finally realized I had had enough. I stared at him and felt as if I were seeing him clearly for the very first time. I shook my head and then spoke calmly, one word at a time. "I….will….not….shut….up." Those five words were the match that sparked the fumes that had been filling his mother's house since we arrived. How dare I speak to him that way! He launched into a physical fury, throwing his arms in the air, making cruel threats, storming around the room. Mama Dot was trying to calm him down, when all of a sudden, he took a deep breath and became quiet and still. It was so eerie that I almost had to remind myself to breathe. What do you do when you have been dropped into the eye of a hurricane? What do you do when the

47

snake in the dark stops rattling but you have to sleep in the house with it that night?

Before I gathered my family to return to the little concrete house, I pulled my mother-in-law aside. "I am afraid," I said aloud for the first time. Tears filled my eyes as I prayed she would hear all the things I could not say. In her sweet way she told me to "go on home and try to work things out." Against my will, the air escaped my lungs in a loud sigh: "What was she talking about? Work things out? This wasn't some lover's spat!" I nodded and turned to leave the room. "Marian," she said almost in a whisper. My eyes were still welled up with tears as I turned to look back at her sweet face. "Turn the porch light on if you need me. I'll be watching." I nodded again and didn't say another word as we left the house. I didn't have a phone, but at least I knew she would be watching and I would be able to signal her.

The drive up to our little house was quiet except for some small talk between the children and myself. Once home, my goal was to get the children down for bed as quickly as possible and then just hope he would drink himself to sleep as he had done so many times before. I tucked the children in and made certain they were all asleep before I left the bedroom. I tried to brace myself for what I knew was coming. If anyone reading this is there now, I ache for you. It is heartbreakingly painful and mere words cannot describe the emptiness and gut-wrenching pain that accompanies feeling so unwanted, so unworthy, so unloved. When you fear for your life in your own home, you experience the same trauma that a soldier feels in battle, only you are unarmed.

When I walked into the living room, he kept his head facing the television and cut his eyes over to me. The reflection of the TV made his eyes glow like the devil. "You know how you humiliated me, talking to me like that in front of my mother?" he began. Soon the yelling was so loud that Dorothy began crying. She was only eleven months old at the time and I picked her up to console her. "Shut her up!" he screamed as he slung the back of his fist into my face with all of his strength. Somehow I was able to keep my balance and not drop Dorothy. "Now I am going to go boil some water," he threatened with his lips pursed and his nostrils flaring. As he went to the kitchen, I locked myself and the children in the bedroom promising myself it would be for the very last time.

I never turned the porch light on that night. I have no idea how long my mother-in-law sat in the dark of her home watching our house.

Chapter 14 Hittin' the road

The next morning, my husband left as if nothing had happened the night before. I walked over to a friend's house who was my co-cohort in one my creative endeavors: making pocketbooks. My husband's mother came to see me and asked what had happened. I gave her the details, which upset her, but I knew there was nothing she could do. "Mama Dot," I said, trying to let her hear the sincerity in my voice, "I will not be living in that house much longer."

That week, I watched as my husband took some of his clothing into the back yard, doused them with lighter fluid and dropped a match. I didn't know if he had lost his mind, was destroying evidence, or both. Either way, as I stood hiding in the curtains watching him through the window, I had no doubts about my next step. I sent the children to their Aunt's that day and they did not get home until he was asleep. It was a Saturday morning as I put Dodie in her stroller - our only wheels for the past 5 years - awoke Sydney and Hunter and we all strolled down to his mother's house. As I stood in her doorway with Dodie's diaper bag hanging from my arm and my children clinging to each leg, I said, "I/we have spent our last night in that house." She looked away as if she simply could not deal with what I was saying. I still hurt for her when I remember that beautiful Saturday morning in the warmth of her kitchen. She had suffered such a great loss just a month before and I knew it would tear her apart to be away from her grandchildren, but I had no choice. "I have to leave for a funeral," she told me. As she moved passed me, she squeezed my arm and made casual conversation with the children in her perky, loving way.

After she left, I went to the phone and called Sue, Beth, and my brother. We began to put a plan together. As luck would have it, my brother was on his way through town heading to his new home in Gainesville, Georgia. He had planned to stop by and see me even before he knew of my emergency plans. I watched as my children's father left for the day to do whatever it was he did all day. I phoned the police and told them about my situation and my plan to stay at my sister-in-laws home until I could leave town. When my husband came up to her house that night, we called the police again. My husband's brother went outside to try to calm my husband and acted as a go-between for the police and the madman who was storming around the yard. "All I want to do is take my son up to the house to work on the garage with me!" he yelled at the police. "Who gives you the right to tell a man what he can and can't do with his own son?" There was absolutely no way I was going to allow him to take any of my children anywhere. I was afraid of what he would do with Hunter, although I still believe his threats were usually just that. But the tide had turned, I had made a public stand against him and I could not risk any more involvement with him. There was no going back now.

When his brother drove him back to our house to keep him from getting a DUI, I saw my chance. I called Sue and Beth and told them to be on the lookout for us. We were on our way. They had already arranged a safe house for us. It wasn't as if I could ask the children for their permission or support in this decision, but they had seen their father's ravings the night before and they seemed to want to get away as badly as I did.

Papa Bill had always been Sydney's protector and with him gone and her Dad showing how unstable he had become, thankfully, she did not have to be persuaded to leave. Her willingness made the experience much easier for me and I thanked God for her willingness to cooperate. I hurt for parents who have to take a child kicking and screaming to safety. It is difficult enough to uproot and leave everything you have ever known, but my children put their complete faith in me. I could not let them down.

Our "safe place" was the last place my husband would ever think to look. We stayed at the home of a friend who was literally a "pistol-packing mama!" I nicknamed her "Thelma" and she reminded me of one of my aunts who would literally shoot through a door first and then ask questions later. My husband had never met Thelma, so he would not even know to look for us at her home. She was strong, impulsive, opinionated, and she loved me and the children. Without her help, I could not have made my escape. She had such a sweet spirit and she told me how happy it had made her that she was there to help us. Money just can't buy friends like that.

It was a very sad time in my life, when years later, I returned to our "safe house" when we lost Thelma to cancer.

The first night at Thelma's, however, a friend drove up who had the same type of car as my husband. It terrified Sydney until she realized it wasn't her dad's car. We were all in a state of shock as we awaited my brother to come by and solidify the plans for us to move in with him and his family. It was the beginning of the end of my husband's terroristic reign over me and our children. I didn't sleep well that night. In fact, I don't think I slept at all. I cried until I couldn't cry anymore, but I thanked God for helping us make it this far and asked Him for strength to never return. I cried with joy as I watched my children sleep. I had finally gotten them out of there! My heart ached and rejoiced at the same time. We stayed hidden for several days. A social worker came by with some games and clothes for the children, which they desperately needed. We had left with only the shirts on our back and Dodie's diaper bag. Our guardian angel named Joanne gave the children kindness and love and saw them through some very difficult days.

I was restless as I waited for Beth and her husband, Michael to take me to Georgia. In nightmares, I'd be walking into the little concrete house. In those dreams, the house had bars on the windows and the door would slam behind me like the lid on a coffin. I would awaken terrified, counting the days. We were almost free.

Chapter 15 Justice

I know a lot about conditioning. I have conditioned my body day and night since I was a child. By repeating certain things over and over, I am able to generate a certain response. As a personal trainer, I watch it work for the good every day. When a client repeats a squat or a bench press over and over, first it creates gentle lines in the arms and legs. Soon, the shapes of muscles appear and the body grows stronger and becomes healthier.

Conditioning, indeed, works for the good, but it can also work to our detriment.

Back in the mid-60s, a psychologist at the University of Pennsylvania was conducting studies using groups of dogs. The study seemed cruel, but what the psychologists learned has helped thousands of people overcome bad conditioning. The researchers randomly assigned dogs to different groups. Two of the groups received the same length and intensity of short jolts of electric shock at the same time. The dogs in one group had the ability to press a lever and put an immediate end to the shock they felt and the shock that was simultaneously delivered to dogs in the other group.

Put yourself in the place of these dogs. What if you felt pain, pressed a lever, and the pain ended? Would you feel empowered? Would you feel hopeful? What if you were a dog in the second group? You don't suffer any more than the dogs in the first group, but the shocks seem random; and regardless of what you do, the shocks just keep coming. Eventually, according to the researchers, the dogs in the second group "learned to be helpless." They would just cower and whimper. Even when the dogs in the second group were later given the opportunity to press a lever which would end their suffering, they had been conditioned over and over to just take it. And that's what they did.

I can relate. When you just keep getting zapped, you begin to lose faith that anything will ever get any better. I had become very skeptical of the legal system; and that cynicism had kept me in my "marriage", and I use that term loosely, much longer than I would have liked or anticipated. Things had been going wrong for so long that I had decided if I tried to change anything it would be a waste of time, or worse, I would lose my children because I had no means of providing for them.

I dreaded the thought of standing before a judge, asking for permission to take my children out of the state so that I could live with my brother. Over and over in the last few years, the "authority" in my life had been abusive and cruel. I had almost come to expect the same from the court system. I had also heard people say that a bad father was better than no father at all. The closer the time came for the emergency hearing, the more anxious I became.

The night before I was to appear in court, my "shoot-first" friends announced they were going to take me shopping. "You need to wear something that's acceptable in a courtroom," they said. I had been wearing my 60-year-old aunt's hand-me-downs for years. She was so sweet to give them to me and I was grateful to have something to wear, but the only way I would have made a good impression in those clothes was if I reminded the judge of his beloved grandmother. Earlier that night I had been worrying that anything I pulled from my suitcase would make me look weak and incapable before the judge. My friends' kindness was more than I could take. When my eyes started to water, they dropped their shoulders and looked away. They were afraid they had hurt my feelings, but it was their gentle kindness that touched me so deeply. How is it that I could take attack after attack from my husband and never shed a tear, but a small act of kindness broke me?

That trip to Walmart felt like a shopping spree on Rodeo Drive! I had not been allowed to go or take the children shopping in years. I would ride along with my mother-in-law from time to time when she invited me, and she did quite often, but if my husband ever took me, I was literally put on a time clock and rushed through so that he could take me and the children back home and then disappear again into the night. When my friends took me to Walmart, I quickly pulled something off the rack and said "I think this will do and it should fit." They laughed and said, "Marian, why don't you get a few things that you like and go try them on to be sure?" They waited patiently as I tried on clothes. They offered wonderful advice about what blouse might go with what jacket. They brought me different skirts and shoes to try on. You would have thought I was the most important person in the world. They sure did make me feel that way.

The next day, in the emergency hearing, I sat and awaited the judge's permission to take my children to Georgia. I was afraid to even let myself dream that it would all go that well. It seemed too good to be true: a new town, a new state, and hopefully a new life with dreams and opportunities for all of us. I sat there in my new Walmart dress and tried to hold myself together. I had no idea how it would go, but like the dogs who just kept feeling jolts of electricity piercing them, I guess I had come to expect the worse, but deep inside, I still hoped for a miracle. When the judge heard that my husband had struck me while I had been holding our infant child, however, it was an open and shut case. I was surprised that my husband did not even try to deny what he had done.

I was also surprised to learn that the person who is fleeing from the other in fear still has to plan the visits with the one they're running from. In our case, it was very difficult to find anyone who wanted to be the supervisor for my estranged husband during such visits.

My husband had burned every bridge he had ever crossed, but his mother stepped up to the plate. That worried me because of his control over her; and honestly, there was nothing she could have done to stop him if he decided to do something crazy. But the judge had granted me sole custody and said that we were free to go to Georgia.

I couldn't believe it. It had worked. Somewhere out in the universe, something had shifted. I had stepped on a lever; and this time, something good had happened. It was one of the most liberating experiences of my life.

Chapter 16 My golden Bi-Lo card

When my friends and I left the courtroom that day, I felt as if I'd received a full pardon and had just stepped outside the prison's concertina wire and gates for the first time in decades. On the way home, we stopped in the local Bi-Lo, and I grabbed a cart. I tried to remember the last time I had been in a grocery store and pushed my own cart. Since the automobile accident, I hadn't been allowed to shop for groceries on my own. Occasionally, my husband would do the shopping, but usually my mother-in-law, brought me things to cook. I was eternally grateful, but I hadn't realized how much I missed the simple pleasures of a grocery store. Sometimes I hear women complaining about how they have to go buy groceries, and when I am slammed busy today I guess I understand. But I don't think I will ever again be able to take such simple freedoms for granted. Could be why I love my local Publix store and the employees that work there so much.

As we moved through Bi-Lo's produce section, I felt like Dorothy on the Yellow Brick Road, the brightly colored tomatoes and peppers cheering me on in high pitched voices. Skip, skip, step-ball-change. The further we moved through the store, the giddier I became. I was on cloud nine.

When we approached the checkout, the cashier asked me, "Do you have your Bi-Lo Bonus Shopping Card with you?" I told her that I didn't have one, and asked how much they cost. "Oh, they are free," she told me as she scanned a loaf of bread. They just help you save money when you shop here." "Then I definitely would like to have one please," I told her. She gave me a little form which I filled out and then she reached in her drawer and handed me a laminated card and a smaller version I could put on my keychain. Of course, I didn't have a key chain, so I just tucked it in my purse and started laughing like a school girl. I had my OWN Bi-Lo shopper's card! You would have thought I had won the lottery, and if I can be perfectly honest, I felt as if I had. I clicked my ruby slippers, grabbed my bags, and leaned in on my friends as we sashayed from the store, light-headed with our own good fortune.

Chapter 17 A brand new start

Gainesville is a beautiful north Georgia town that's known its share of tragedy. It burned to the ground in 1851. In 1936, two funnel clouds met downtown creating a deadly tornado that left hundreds dead and the shops and businesses in a pile of bricks and twisted metal. Storm winds from the 1936 tornado carried letters from Gainesville over 67 miles away to Anderson, South Carolina, my hometown. It was such a significant event that even today, young children in the town can tell you about it. When the sky turns yellow and hail falls on a hot spring day, all of the old-timers have a story to tell from when they were young; and those stories still shape the culture of Gainesville.

My brother had given me directions to his home in Georgia; and on a gorgeous Thursday my special friends drove me and my children down historic Green Street toward our new home. I felt an instant kinship with the town. Green Street's four lanes are frighteningly narrow to minimize the impact the road makes on the yards of the beautiful antebellum homes. Old oaks shade the large white houses, most of which are now office buildings for dentists, lawyers and real estate agents. I rolled down the window, closed my eyes, and let the fresh air of this new town tangle my hair and fill my lungs.

My brother's family had not even moved to Gainesville when they all agreed we could stay in their home until I was able to get back on my feet. I will forever be indebted to them all for their graciousness and generosity in our time of need. They were still living in North Carolina so that their children could finish the school year before moving to Gainesville. Unfortunately, waiting to finish the school year was not an option for me, so the doctor who had cared for me during my pregnancy with Dodie helped me arrange for the children to be dismissed from school before the year ended.

When we arrived in my brother's empty house, I had a haunting memory of the move back to my childhood home after my first marriage had ended. I missed my dad deeply and felt the two funnel clouds of self-loathing and fear headed straight for me. Here I was again, picking up the pieces after a marriage to the wrong man. Luckily, Sydney saved me from my dark thoughts with a squeal of delight as she danced around the room, happy to be getting a new start. I grinned at her, put down my boxes, and danced right along with her.

One of my favorite Mary Kay Ash sayings was "fake it 'til you make it." So I pretended I wasn't afraid of what was ahead of me. In the next few weeks, I had a long "to-do" list that was daunting to say the least: find work, find an apartment, find childcare, arrange visitation for my children with a man who terrified me, start driving again, and re-learn practically everything I had ever learned to be able to make decisions for myself.

Sometimes, those decisions were absolutely overwhelming. In the little concrete house, every choice was made for me. Now, I felt as if my brain short-circuited every time I was faced with more than one option. Maybe I was terrified that my choice would be wrong, or maybe I was just out of practice. I'm not sure which, but I know that if it had not been for Sue and Beth, I would not have accomplished anything. In phone call after phone call, my faithful friends would tell me what they'd do in my situation and then always end the conversation saying, "But Marian, you can make your own decision. You can do this." Maybe that's what I needed more than their advice: someone telling me they believed in me.

In the experiment from the 1960s where the scientists shocked the dogs and gave birth to the term "learned helplessness," some dogs quickly learned to overcome their bad programming. The observers determined that certain dogs were just more optimistic by nature and were able to work their way out of a bad circumstance in spite of their experiences. In more than one instance in my life, friends had joked that I am like the little boy who spends his days shoveling through manure saying "there's got to be a pony in here somewhere." I was counting on that eternal optimism and my faith to help me through the rough days ahead. It wasn't going to be easy, but all around me in this wonderful new town was a spirit that said it's possible to grieve terrible losses and rebuild after a storm.

Chapter 18 A hand up, not a hand out

In the parking lot of the Department of Family and Children Services, I closed my eyes, whispered a prayer, straightened my shoulders and swallowed the pride that stuck in my throat like a huge multi-vitamin turned sideways. When I walked through those doors, I was about to become a welfare mother. I felt guilty that I needed help and then guilty that I had a stereotype of "welfare mother." I didn't want to be there, but I was on a mission. I had to get back up and running...and fast. I remember sitting in that little concrete house wondering how would I make it and this just happened to be my first step. I needed to crawl before I could walk and then with God on my side, surely I would be able to run again someday.

Once inside, I began filling out the forms that I hoped would help me find suitable training and provide for my family until I was gainfully employed. I talked with some of the other people who were waiting with me. Most of them, like me, were single mothers. Statistically, well over 90 percent of welfare recipients are single moms, most of whom receive no child support and many of whom are employed full-time in low-wage jobs. Some of the women fit the image I had in my mind as they complained about the time they had to wait to see someone. Others I identified with more quickly. They didn't like being there anymore than I did and would prefer never to take a handout. They were grateful that the help was available, however, and if they hated the wait, they kept it to themselves. Merissa, Bobbie and the other women who worked in the DFACs office treated me with respect and spoke in loving tones to me and my children. Their compassion made what would have been a humiliating experience almost bearable. Those girls in that office may never know how their kindness made me feel human again, but I hope they realize how very special they are.

Through DFACs, I received my second "shopping card." The little debit card look-alike spared me the shame of looking like I was carrying "food stamps" when I reached the checkout counter to buy my groceries. I surely didn't want anyone to notice and look at me with pity. I tried to make the very best of the support I received. I clipped coupons, bought generic, and planned my meals down to the last detail so that nothing was wasted. I was one frugal mama!

I also received support from Gainesville's local battered women's shelter, The Gateway House. Though I never stayed as a resident at the shelter, the children and I attended weekly group meetings. I would go to the adult class and the children would go with counselors to the children's group. Going to a battered women's shelter was almost as humbling as applying for welfare. The women in the group came from every walk of life. The counselor told us how important it was that no one knows the location of the shelter to protect the women and children who stay there. She also instructed us to hold each other's identities in the strictest confidence. I sat back and listened as women shared details of their own personal nightmares. I was shocked by the similarities in our stories, though some were even worse than my own.

One woman, a young petite brunette with a tattoo of a butterfly on her wrist admitted to being as abusive as her partner. "If he hits me, I hit him back," she blurted as she leaned back and slid down in her chair with her arms crossed in front of her. "Ya'll are crazy if you just take it." Then a beautiful, obviously wealthy woman with a sparkling tennis bracelet and french manicure lifted her eyes to meet the young brunette's. She sat with her shoulders back and her head so still we could all almost see the imaginary book that sat on top of her perfectly coifed head. Only her lips moved as she spoke in a soft Southern drawl, "If I lift a hand, he will kill me." Around the room, heads nodded.

From week to week new members would be added to the group. Some disappeared and I never saw them again. The counselor at the Gateway House told us that most women in abusive situations return to their partners eight or more times before finally leaving for good. Some, unfortunately, leave in a body bag.

It was mind-boggling. Even with the struggles I was facing, I could not imagine going back to the life I had before. Thanks to God's help and the support of my friends and family, when I left the little house for the last time, I knew I would never go back. As in the DFACs office, I found myself swinging from judging these women to empathizing with them. I'd think, "I would never have put up with that," then hear someone say the same thing about my story. Sitting in the group, listening to the progressive nature of the abuse experienced by everyone there, I knew I had made the right choice. That didn't mean it wouldn't be hard, and believe you me, it was; but I knew in my heart that leaving him was the best decision I had ever made.

Chapter 19 "Indy"

Since 1997, my only wheels had been a baby stroller. I was delighted when my brother loaned me a car so that I could find suitable child care for Dodie and attend the computer classes offered by the Department of Children and Family Services. I was heading home from class one afternoon when a car t-boned my car. In a form of post traumatic stress disorder, I was terribly anxious about the loss of the car for my brother and for myself. "Not again," I remember thinking during the moments just after the car hit me. I awoke to see my brother standing over me in the emergency room. "Don't worry about it Sis," he said, holding up his hand and cutting off my apologies before I could speak. "It wasn't your fault and at least you are okay."

Since I had moved to Gainesville, I had two priorities: find suitable day care for Dodie and find a job. It was really all I could think about. I didn't have time to be hurt. I looked around the ER and promptly pulled out two copies of my resume which I shared with different attendants. "You sure are persistent," my brother chuckled.

Later that week, my mom kindly offered me some money from my father's trust fund so that I could find a used car. I was excited to have a car of my own and terrified by the weight of the decision. When I found a car I thought I could afford, I took it to a shop for a mechanic's opinion and then made the dealer an offer. The children and I loved that car and decided to name it "Indy" for Independence.

On weekends, we'd ride around looking for an apartment and sometimes drive by nicer homes, too. I'd say to myself and sometimes out loud, "I can't afford you yet, but I sure do deserve to live in you." The kids and I would laugh and plan aloud about our dream home. From the size of the yard to the color of the walls, we planned every detail. It was a silly mind game we played. I couldn't afford any home on my own yet, and it really didn't matter. The little taste of freedom that I'd experienced was so sweet that I knew if we had to live in a tent, we could do it and be happy.

Chapter 20 Freedom isn't always free

There's a big problem with independence. "Freedom", as they say, "isn't really and truly free." Our car, Indy, was such a blessing, thanks to a gift of money from my mom. Because I couldn't afford a car payment, I knew I had to get a high mileage older car. Indy was much better than walking; but not long after we bought the car, things started to go wrong under the hood. That's the way of independence: you think "Wow! I've made it" with some delusion that now everything is going to be perfect. When Indy finally became more expensive to keep than I could possibly afford, I sat in the driver's seat, pounding the stirring wheel. How could I ever come up with enough money each month to pay on another car?

Slavery has its benefits I guess. In the little concrete house, I didn't have to worry about how I'd get to work... or how I'd get anywhere for that matter. I just couldn't and didn't go anywhere. I didn't have to worry about whether or not I did the right thing with every penny like I had to now. Back then, I didn't have even one penny to my name.

Indy's windshield wipers squeaked across the windshield as I sat in the pouring rain lamenting my problems. "Okay," I said aloud. The sound of my own voice startled me as it echoed around the car. "I am never going to have a problem-free life, but the quality of my problems certainly has improved!" I nursed the car home and resigned myself to the reality of a car payment when I had no idea what I could possibly give up in order to make that happen.

Over the next few months, I completed my computer training at the technical school and landed a job as Director of Sports Marketing with the local Convention and Visitor's Bureau. I felt as if I was made for this particular job or it was made for me. Whatever the case, I was back into promoting athletics and working with a caring, professional group of people who treated me with respect. I was on my way back up and it felt great.

Chapter 21 Peace in the present

Early one Saturday morning I was sitting on the bed reading. The kids were all asleep, and the two-bedroom apartment we'd rented was unusually quiet. I looked up from the pages of the book and stared at the dark small room where my clothes lived when I was not wearing them. Normally, a voice inside me would start scolding because I had left my running shoes piled just outside the closet rather than neatly in their place. I had come to know that the voice belonged to someone who no longer had power over me, but sometimes his critiques drowned out the gentle voice of reason. As I stared at the closet in the quiet of the apartment, for just a moment, my closet was beautiful to me. It was full of hand-me-downs and finds from the local Potter's House, but the colors were so nice. One skirt was hung wrong, too close to the skirts beside it and it stood out from the row I usually kept perfectly in place. The dress from Walmart which I'd worn to the emergency hearing hung near the center. I was entranced by the calm of the apartment and the balance of the asymmetry in my closet. Soon the critic in my head would resurrect himself, and I'd have to put the shoes away and straighten the skirt on its hanger; but for a very brief moment of clarity, I was not my body, my clothes, my apartment or my car (or lack thereof). Those fleeting moments sometimes moved across me like a soft breeze and then they'd be gone; but when I was in them, I was gently assured that I am eternal and infinitely precious regardless of my imperfections.

The apartment we'd moved to after I had found work was small but cozy. We'd chosen a gated community, which under the circumstances I felt was best. We were living life at a frantic pace. We started before dawn as I drove Sydney and Hunter to school, dropped Dodie off at day care, then on to work for me. I loved my work, but by the time I returned home, the moments with my children seemed much too short. They'd work on homework while I prepared dinner. Sometimes we'd play outside or pile together in the living room floor in front of the television a friend had given us. Most nights by the time I drug myself into bed after laundry and cleaning up, I was completely exhausted. All the work aside, life was wonderful! When I locked the doors at night, I didn't live in fear of drunken, perverse ravings or unwarranted beatings. I poured myself out every day until there was literally nothing left in me and then welcomed the rest that comes after a long, hard day of work. The bed I slept in was one of my proud creations: fashioned from the frame of a bunk bed that members of our new church had given me and a mattress I found for $15. After I thought I had Lysol-ed, beaten and treated it sufficiently, the used mattress on the wired together bunk bed became a haven to me.

Sometimes, as the children would drift off to sleep, I would sit in the quiet and darkness and cry my eyes out. I fell to my knees and thanked God for giving me these children and for protecting them in the wreck so many years ago and making it possible for me to get them to safer ground. Sometimes, all of the emotions of when I had been trapped in the little concrete house would play through my mind. I would remember all of the times I sat in that house and asked myself, "how will I ever be able to get out of here; and if I do, how in the heck will I be able to take care of these three children and give them a happy life?"

Things in my closet and my life were a bit messy but that was okay. That's how people really are, regardless of how hard we try to line everything up, exercise everything to perfection, press out all the wrinkles and pretend otherwise. In the end, we are all imperfectly perfect.

Chapter 22 Our lullaby

One night when we were living in the concrete house, I was awakened by Dorothy's frightened cry. More than just a whimpering or whining, she was obviously in some kind of severe discomfort. I tried to make sure she was awake and not dreaming of something that had frightened her. She tightened her little body, threw her head back and continued to wail. I searched her from head to toe for a bug bite or mark to give me some idea of what was causing her to cry. Dorothy had always been my best sleeper, but she was inconsolable this night. I tried every trick God has ever given mothers to calm their young. Nothing worked. I was rocking her and humming tried-and-true lullabies as she continued to sob. Eventually, I was writing tunes of my own and soon she began to be soothed. I am not gifted as a singer, but a baby loves the sound of her mother's voice. Dorothy's cries turned to sniffling and eventually silence so that she could hear me hum. In the days that followed, the tune I hummed grew into a song that we now affectionately call "Our Lullaby."

The song became my most powerful tool in getting the children to sleep before their dad staggered in. I had convinced myself that the song had magical powers because of the soothing effect it had on my children. When we were living in my brother's home and after we got our own apartment, I continued to sing the song to them at night. Some nights, because I was so exhausted, I would fall asleep before I finished all three verses, but it served its purpose. It gave us all a sense of peace and tranquility that we all longed for.

Starting over had created a time of real loneliness for me, although I really had not had a husband in all of my years with their father. It was a strange thing to think of myself as lonely since I was very happy

71

surrounded by the love of my children. So in the duration, our lullaby comforted me as much as it soothed the children in those early times after we were on our own.

It surprised me how a man's attention at work or church would brighten my mood. Once, a man with a beautiful British accent called where I worked. We began a friendship and dated for a while. He was thoughtful and attentive, but eventually we decided we should go our own ways. I still remember him fondly and feel gratitude to him to this day that I had the privilege of knowing him. He gave me the shot of confidence that I had long-since lost and through his kindness, I began to feel desirable again and it was a good feeling. But then there were times when I met men who seemed to be interested, that I felt as though I was merely viewed as a liability.

Honestly, during those days as I was coming out of the dark, I felt that way with everyone around me except my children. I was certain that men had a ledger that put beauty and sex appeal on a huge scale next to the responsibility that came along with a woman with children. In my eyes, when they weighed my value, I wasn't worth the effort. Sometimes I would forget that there are men who value family and are willing to sacrifice themselves for the rewards that come with being committed and fully connected. That faulty thinking caused me to short-change myself and my children. No doubt there are men who would only see me and my kids as a burden; but if I had taken the time to really assess things, I would have seen my thinking as a lie from the adversary of my soul. How could anyone who I'd want in our lives possibly see the children as anything less than the precious creations they were? If a man did not want to know and love them, then I should have seen that as a built-in filter for screening my dates. I should have been grateful for the wall of protection God put between me and men who would see me as property to be purchased and my children as only unwanted responsibility.

In those lonely days when I longed for the company of a man but felt as though no man could possibly want to be with me, I needed the gift of Our Lullaby. "Someday," I'd tell the kids, "I am going to be on Oprah and Faith Hill is going to sing our song." That may sound like a silly pipe dream, but I believe in dreaming big. It would be sad to know I went through my entire life afraid to give voice to my dreams even if they are highly improbable. You really just don't know until you try.

With my dream of Faith singing our song in mind, I made a copy of the song and sent it to myself via certified mail. When the letter came to me "from me", I joyfully signed on the line and thanked the carrier for making my day. "Look kids," I shouted, waving the envelope like we'd just received a lottery check: "It's our song!"

The envelope is still unopened, a constant reminder of our family dream of better things to come. I still sing the song to them. Sydney and Hunter's voices are now far superior to my own and their infatuation and need for me has changed as they move toward and through adolescence; but Dorothy still asks me to sing "our song" to her most every night. And yes, we still dream together.

Photo Gallery

The children in Uncle Dave's front yard 1 month after we moved to Gainesville, Ga. (2002)

Sydney helping Papa Bill with his present she gave to him. Her Uncle Donnie is looking on.

Copy of the envelope I sent to myself "certified mail" back in April 2006. My dream then was to go on The Oprah Winfrey Show and have Faith Hill sing "Our Lullaby."

The kids and me in June 2008.

Me and the rest of the team during my early days at the local YMCA pool. I am in the first row, second from the left.

Dear Becka

I saw our beautiful, elegant Marian on the Oprah show last week......first of all, I couldn't
believe that I knew anyone that had the poise to be there talking to millions. I was so
impressed and fascinated.

Marian has always been my 4th child...I love her dearly and as you remember well, we
spent countless hours together. I'm so sorry that her life has been so difficult, but
equally, I'm so proud of her, her strength to keep her family together and be financially
independent. That takes "guts".

Marian, you and Earle have had a strong influence on our lives. Gary has loved you all
and misses the connection, distance and support. She was/is his older "sister". I see you
and Earle in Marian...intelligent, self confidant, creative, fun loving, supportive true
friend. You know swimming was the sport that instilled self confidence in their
bodies.....I can just hear you say with a sparkle in your eye "if you got it, flaunt it". I
loved/love your humor. Who knew that Marian would earn a living by keeping her body
fit or Gary get up every morning for work at 5 am because of what they grew up
enjoying/doing.

I hope your wrist is well and you are going strong again in all the things you enjoy.
We've been adding on to the lake house....a bedroom and a bath so I can get through the
doors. Gary, Kim and kiddos will come for Easter weekend.......where will you be? Tell
Susan hello.

Take care and know we love you,
Winnie

The letter I received from Miss Winnie following my appearance on The
Oprah Winfrey Show.

Me as I began living my dream of being a Personal Fitness and Life Coach.

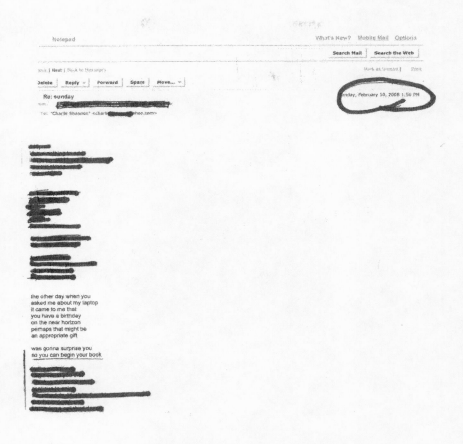

the other day when you
asked me about my laptop
it came to me that
you have a birthday
on the near horizon
perhaps that might be
an appropriate gift

was gonna surprise you
so you can begin your book

Email I got from Mick stating his intent to get me a laptop so I could begin to write my book. (This email came <u>2</u> <u>days</u> before I ever got the first call from the staff at The Oprah Winfrey Show.)

Sydney, Hunter, and Dorothy. Together at the beach. (2009)

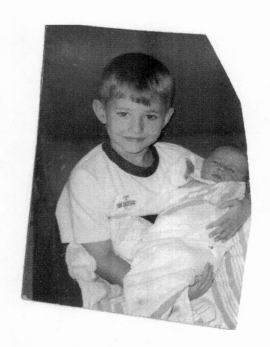

Hunter holding his baby sister, Dorothy, for the very first time. (2001)

Chapter 23 Giving thanks

One Friday evening, I heard a knock on the apartment door. I expected a neighbor coming to chat, but as the door swung open, I saw my ex-husband standing there smiling as if I should be glad to see him.

"Hey, baby, I thought I'd come see you and the kids," he said as he slid past me and into the living room. I don't know why I hadn't expected this; but in my mind, I had treated the Georgia state line as if it were the Atlantic Ocean and he'd have to swim across it to find me.

After a brief period of awkwardness, the children were glad to see their dad. They told him about their teachers, new friends, and whatever else he asked them about. Sydney asked about Mama Dot and her aunts and uncles. As I sat watching him be so kind to the kids, I started to second-guess myself. Maybe it wasn't as bad as I had thought. Maybe he had changed.

I snapped right out of that delusion when he asked me for money.

My head rocked back on my neck as if he'd just punched me again. He paid no child support, helped in no way with the care of our children, had neglected, abused and mistreated us for years, but he knew I had a job now and saw me as an easy mark. I told him I only had thirty dollars in cash, but he was welcome to it if he'd just go away.

I went to my purse hoping there was one decent bone in his body and that he would not take his children's grocery money. I knew that I shouldn't give it to him. At the same time, in a strange way, it was worth it. As soon as I saw his hands taking the money from mine, I was completely recommitted to live a life without him.

Later that weekend, I received a call from the emergency room telling me that my husband had fallen in the shower of a local hotel room.

Visions of my ex-husband's ravings about "a big settlement" following my automobile accident flashed through my mind. "If only you and the kids had been hurt worse," he had said. The voice of the nurse from the emergency room repeated my name. "Yes," I said. "I am still here. Thank you for calling me, but I think you need to call his mother. He is my estranged husband and I am not responsible for him." I hung up the phone and sat wondering if he'd really fallen or was trying to come up with some quick money. I prayed he wasn't terribly hurt and hated pawning him off on his sweet mother, but he simply could not be my problem anymore. Deep inside, I knew that he was trying to find a way back into my life. I simply could not let that happen.

I learned later that he received a small settlement from the hotel and had blown it quickly without paying the bills he had built up. Though he tormented me briefly saying that he had a great job in Gainesville and would be moving down soon, his plans never materialized and the kids and I had a smooth, peaceful couple of months.

As Thanksgiving approached, we planned for the older two children to visit with him overnight. I would bring Dodie by for a visit and then take the kids with me to my sister's home. The Friday after Thanksgiving, Dodie and I drove up to Mama Dot's. She threw open her arms and welcomed us to her home which still smelled of her turkey and dressing from the day before. I leaned against the kitchen counter and watched, with great joy, as Dodie and Mama Dot covered each other with love and affection.

It was nice to be back in Mama Dot's house. Things never changed there. Long after Papa Bill was gone, you could still feel his presence in every room. Of course, my ex-husband was the perfect picture of a gentleman. He was attentive with the children and patient with his mother. But it was easier to be strong here. The little concrete house just up the hill was like a magnet painfully drawing out the shards of memories from my brain. That night, I slept with one eye open and never would have dreamed what would happen in the morning. When I woke, it was in a panic to the sound of Sydney screaming.

I ran in my bare feet to the top of the basement stairs. At the bottom of the steps lay Mama Dot as grey as the concrete floor beneath her. I flew down the stairs to her. She was conscious but complaining of nausea. Together, her son and I helped her into the shower. I stepped in, still in my pajamas. "Does anything hurt?" I asked her. She was obviously weak and shaken. The water washed over her and dripped from her hair, cheeks and the tip of her nose. She looked in my eyes and told me she was sore and bruised from the fall, but had no real pain other than that. Over the next few minutes, she seemed to improve. We got her into bed and all decided that she must have just stumbled. I dressed quickly and ran to her brother's house to let them know we thought she needed to go to the emergency room.

After my ex-husband and Mama Dot left to have her checked at the hospital, I loaded the kids in the car and headed over to my sister's for our Thanksgiving time together. The kid's dad had wanted to take the children with him to the hospital, but that was no place for them to be. The next day on the way home to Georgia, I answered my phone to learn that Mama Dot had passed away. I tried to keep myself together as I pulled over to the side of the road and began crying. I knew that my reaction would upset the kids, but with tears streaming down my cheeks I told the children that their grandmother had gone to be with Papa Bill. We all sat there and cried together. Mama Dot was such a good lady. She had worked so hard all of her life and had loved us and cared for us when her son had not. We said a prayer together to thank God for giving us this special time with Mama Dot and for bringing us back to her home to see her this one last time.

We drove back up to South Carolina for her funeral later that week, but an ice storm warning meant we had to leave just after the visitation. The children said good-bye to their dad, and he promised he would come see them. I didn't put much stock in that promise and I hoped the kids didn't either. As young as they were, they were beginning to see through his lies. As we were walking out of the funeral home, my former brother-in-law told me that Mama Dot had already shopped for the kids' Christmas gifts and asked if his brother could bring them down to us. "That would mean a lot to the kids," I said. I hugged him and we left for Georgia.

Very late one night in the following weeks, my estranged husband called and asked if he could bring the presents by for the kids. I told him they were already in bed and asked if he could possibly come after they got home from school the next day. He appeared agitated with me, but I simply could not open up our sanctuary to him that late at night. We didn't hear from him the next day, or the next. Christmas came and went. We have not heard from him since that phone call in December of 2002.

In the days after I told him he couldn't bring the presents, I second guessed myself repeatedly. Was I the reason he didn't come the next day? Would the kids ever see their dad again? And if not, was that my fault?

Mama Dot's presents never made it to our house, but it was the first year, in over five years, that I was able to go to a store and buy my children a gift all on my own. I asked a friend from church to come over late one night to stay with the kids, and I drove over to the K-mart near our apartment. I wasn't able to get them much, but everything I pulled from the shelf and put in my buggy filled me with such joy. That was a Christmas with small gifts but lots of love and lots of laughter. I was in Heaven!

Chapter 24 Elle and 19 cents

Five years of life as a prisoner and the stress of life as a single mom had taken its toll on my body. I was not overweight and had relatively good health, but I knew I wasn't my best. I had brought a Sports Illustrated photo of Elle MacPherson from South Carolina to Georgia with me. It was from the 1987 Swim Suit edition, and though it was tattered and wrinkled, it became my inspiration. One day, just as a joke, I told the kids that it was a photo of me from back in the day; and that I was going to exercise to get back into shape like I was in 1987. I was only teasing when I said it, but the fact that they believed me gave me a shot of confidence to make getting into shape a reality. So, with the tattered image of Elle on my bathroom wall to motivate me, I'd take all three children and head up to the fitness center in the apartment complex. I would climb on the treadmill or the stepper and the children would play right beside me. The conditions weren't ideal. I had hoped that exercising would be a de-stressor for me, but with the kids so close by, I can't say that ever happened. Sometimes they'd get on the treadmill and ride it like a conveyor belt. I'd laugh and then get them safely off the equipment. They'd get restless and I'd stop to get them re-focused on a card game or book, then get back to my workout. We'd head off to the fitness center in rain, sleet, or snow. They were so patient with me; because I guess they wanted their mom to look like Elle again.

I met a neighbor, Charlene, who loved to walk, and she and I became best pals and the speed demons of the apartment complex. In nice weather, we'd plop Dodie in the stroller and set off around the complex. Poor Charlene didn't have my long legs, so she had to work twice as hard to keep up, but she was so much fun to walk with. She was such a caring friend. If she didn't see my light on in the morning when it should be, to make sure

I was up and got the children ready for school, she wouldn't hesitate to call and get me going. We talked non-stop while we power-walked around the apartment complex. Well, to be totally honest, I probably did most of the talking and Charlene, "bless her heart" was an excellent listener. I probably owe that woman millions of dollars for the therapy she provided. Her husband, Carlton, would tease us saying that Dodie was going to grow up to be a race car driver because we were giving her "the need for speed" as we wheeled her around the turns in the complex.

One Saturday, as I was attending one of the children's soccer games, another soccer mom told me of an insurance company that was looking for a new salesperson. I enjoyed my work with the CVB, but knew I needed an opportunity to make more money to provide for my growing family. I promptly went to the interview and got the nod. I didn't know anything about insurance, but the precious lady chosen to be my mentor did such a great job training me that I passed my exam on the very first try. Not to mention, Charlene was a big-wig in the insurance industry, herself and could answer any question I ever had. In fact, she probably had forgotten more about insurance than I would ever know, but she was patient and so helpful. I always thought how cool it was that God had hand-picked Charlene to be my friend at just the time I needed her the most. God is good that way.

My boss, who was a wonderful man, told me that in a year, we would sit down again and discuss my progress and plan a strategy from there. I appreciated the trust they were placing in me and was determined to do a good job for them. I was proud and so was everyone else that I met in that special place. Each person in the office was a blessing to me. I was treated with respect, worked hard to meet their high expectations, and felt like a part of a strong team. I was making a little more money than in my previous job, but as the children grew, their expenses were increasing faster than my pay.

One afternoon as I was leaving work, I pulled into the bank parking lot and walked up to the ATM to check my balance. I stood there on that beautiful fall day and read the faint grey print at the bottom of the receipt: "Balance: $0.19." I stared at the receipt in my hand and then at my reflection in the glass that covered the security camera on the ATM. I was surprised to see that I didn't look like I felt. In fact, I was doing a pretty good job of hiding my situation, even from myself. In the reflection, I saw someone walking up behind me, so I was forced to move out of their way. I was grateful for the reason to take my eyes off of my own reflection. I was working full-time, had no savings, was squeezing every penny, and I had nineteen cents to my name. Now it wasn't like I was surprised by this startling fact. I knew I didn't have any money in the bank before I pulled into the parking lot. It was just the fact of looking at it in print made it seem too real. Almost in a trance, I walked back to my car and thought of my options: I could talk to my brother or mother again for help. I could talk to the man I had just begun dating. The next few minutes seemed like hours as I weighed every possible alternative, and I knew in my heart that I couldn't ask anyone for help again. Having so little money was excruciatingly painful and embarrassing, but it was my reality.

As I sat there is my car, overcome with despair and tears flowing like a river, I prayed once again to God for strength. I had come so far that I couldn't admit defeat now. My brain was swirling and I cried out for some kind of answer and then out of the blue, I heard these faint words ring in my head, "The Nineteen Cent Millionaire." The thought came to me so clearly that if I hadn't been seated in my car I would have surely fallen to the ground. "That's what I am. Yes, that's what I am and that's what I'll name my book." Yes, the absolute thought came to me that somehow I was going to make it out of this financial hole and I was going to write a book to tell others how to stay positive in the face of adversity. It seemed like an odd thought when I was in the depths of despair, but it was crystal clear to me.

As my tears begin to dry, I said aloud, "That's what I am." I have only nineteen cents to my name, but I am still the richest woman alive. I said it to myself over and over, as I tried to convince myself of its truth. But I didn't really believe it. Not yet anyway.

Chapter 25 New faces

I didn't know it, but my time in the little concrete house had given me a "Please, please love me" tattoo that I knew nothing about. I didn't know about the mark it had made on me the day I met Mick. I was actually feeling pretty good and naively confident about how strong I had become. Several months had passed since the day in the bank parking lot. I had saved up enough to take the kids out to eat at a local all-you-can eat buffet. They were so excited as they went through the line loading up their plates with their favorites. Sydney was our ice cream critic and this restaurant had soft serve on their dessert bar. Papa Bill used to take her to the same kind of restaurant back in South Carolina so the restaurant was a mini-homecoming to her. As the kids bounced to their seats in our booth, I thought about how confident and secure they had become since our move to Georgia. It was a welcomed sight to me. I had finally done something right.

The kids kept getting up to go back to the bar, and I had no idea they were making a new friend when one of the children stopped to talk to a stranger who was sitting alone reading a book and eating his supper. "Where is your mother?" Mick asked. She pointed to me and the two of them walked over to our table. We all introduced ourselves and I invited him to join us. "Where is your daddy?" he asked the children. Before I could comment, one of the children said loudly, "there isn't one!" I was a little embarrassed, but I just smiled at him and he smiled back.

We talked a while longer and exchanged business cards. I was flattered by the attention of this man, and it felt good to think that I just might be desirable to him.

For his birthday, Hunter wanted to go back to the all-you-can eat buffet, so I saved for a few weeks then splurged to allow him his wish. We had our dinner and as we were leaving, we ran into the same man we'd met at the restaurant nearly a year earlier. He called himself Mick and we all smiled and said hello. We chatted for a minute, and as I turned to walk out the door, he said, "I'm still single." I was taken aback by his comment, but I turned to reply, "Well, so am I" and we went our separate ways. This time, I received an email from him the very next day. I was so flattered by his attention, but my life was crazy. Any single mother who is solely responsible for the financial provision and care of her children understands what I mean. Work gobbled up the bulk of my days. I had made exercise a priority and that was several hours a week. I had to help children with homework, clean house, do laundry, get the car serviced, everything myself. How was I going to add someone else into my life?

For about a month, Mick would come over around the time the kids were going to sleep. Mick had been through a divorce years earlier and had vowed to be a recluse. He was completely up front with me: he didn't ever see himself as a traditional husband/daddy. I was up front with him as well: I was terrified of anyone ever having that kind of involvement in my life. I genuinely thought, at that time, that maybe we would be able to make it work - not the way most couples did - but in a way that could work for both of us.

Among my photos from those early days in Gainesville is a snapshot of Dodie, passed out into a plate of lasagna. Making my mom's lasagna for the kids had become a tradition for our Christmases together in our new life. That particular holiday, Mom had come to be with the kids, and it was good to have her around. The kids thoroughly enjoyed her company, and we all looked forward to every aspect of the season.

Mama Dot and Papa Bill had always made sure the kids had presents at Christmas. They filled the day with surprises; and even their father, in his own way, got into the spirit. Christmas with a single mom was significantly different, and I had a lot of guilt about that. A friend told me a story about how she'd used an old game system box to wrap a sweater for her son without even thinking about it. "To me it was just a box," she told me, still visibly hurt by the memory of something that had happened years before. "It was just a box a neighbor had told me I could use for wrapping presents. I didn't even know what the darn thing was!" She shook her head and dropped her chin, "I can still see my son's face as he realized that he wasn't getting a game system, but a new sweater instead. I watched him try to hide his disappointment. He was getting a stupid sweater for Christmas, and he was trying to take care of my feelings!" My heart broke for her as she told the story.

Everyone wants to make Christmas special for their children. By observation, Mick had learned enough about us to know that Christmas would NOT be about big presents at our house. He told me things he'd like to do for the children, but I asked him not to. He initially respected my request, but said he really wanted to get the kids some nice presents. I acquiesced because the truth is, I wanted him to I guess, but more than that, I wanted the children to have something nice, as well, for a change. In hindsight, I opened up a can of worms I wish I had not tapped in to, and though I didn't allow myself to think about it as buying their affection or that it might confuse them about his role in their life, I allowed it to happen. How do you know if a line you've drawn is a healthy boundary or if you are motivated by pride? I struggled with it; but at the time, I decided not to fight it and allowed myself to become tangled in the ribbons and laughter that surrounded Mick with my children. I was completely elated as I watched the kids ripping off wrapping paper. I saw how it delighted Mick to make them laugh. I know he gave the presents from his heart, and I know they loved the attention and feelings of approval. I also know that I allowed a shift to begin that Christmas. By not drawing some boundaries that would have meant a leaner Christmas for us, I started allowing Mick to take on small pieces of the role of "dad". He wasn't their dad and had told me, very clearly, that he did not want to start over raising kids. In the fairy tale brewing in my mind, however, a wonderful prince rides in and rescues the damsel, buys beautiful presents for her children, and takes away a little of the fear. It wasn't a happily-ever-after fantasy. I didn't dare dream that the prince would also love, really love, the damsel and her children. Fairy tales like that are just too good to be true, aren't they?

Early the next year, Mick cheerfully took Sydney to a local "Father-Daughter Dance." We bought her a beautiful dress and Mick sported a tux. It meant the world to Sydney. For a child who is growing up without a dad, the chance to have someone step into the story, take you out and say to the world, "this one's mine," is a wonderful thing. I allowed my heart to dream a little that night as I watched them head out. I imagined Sydney with a dad who liked to hear her long, silly stories. I imagined her with a dad who would calm me down when she was going through the crazies of adolescence. I dreamed of our family being normal for once.

Immediately following the Daddy-Daughter dance, however, Mick began to pull back. I was shocked by his attitude; but at the same time, I completely understood it. Mick already had financial obligations from a previous relationship; he was in his mid 50s and had already done the family thing. Before we met, he was dreaming of leaving his practice, moving to Florida and renting lounge chairs on the beach. He was longing for a life with fewer responsibilities, not more of them. I got it. I guess I just didn't like it.

We didn't see each other for several months, but I thought of him all the time and sometimes wondered if any man would be crazy enough to think we were worth the investment. I knew that in the deepest trenches of the ocean of my soul there was a bloody war ravaging me from the inside out. Sometimes, I could almost hear the nineteen cents jingling in my pocket even though I had finally saved a few hundred dollars. When I slowed down long enough, I could hear the whisper as it bubbled up from the abyss, "I'm still here. You can't run from me." In one moment, I was confident of my value as a person just because God had made me and loved me and that was enough. I had a lot going for me and I knew it. But in the next milli-second, I felt fragile, foolish, and worthless. For the most part, I refused to explore the recesses that were home to the whispers. I have learned ways to quiet the echoes: a good day at work is a great ego boost. When someone flirted with me, that was good for a least a couple of days. Mark Twain said he could live for two months on a good compliment. I had him beat. I could feast on a half-hearted compliment even longer. But the darkness was always there, fear of what would happen if I was sick and couldn't work, the fury that no matter how hard I tried, I couldn't scrape together any savings for an emergency fund. I yelled into the depths sometimes, with the bravado of a child humming in the dark, "I can do this!" For months at a time, pretending to be brave seemed to work, so I decided to fake it 'til I could make it just a little longer. Besides I just didn't have the time or the energy for the fight with those demons, figure out where they came from or decide if they were telling the truth.

Eventually, our loneliness won out; and Mick and I reconnected. We both admitted we had missed each other. We talked openly about how we wanted our relationship to progress. He reiterated that he had no desire to be a traditional husband and father. The roles had no appeal to him and made him feel trapped. First and foremost for me at the time, was that I remain independent. I had been dependent on my last husband for everything, and I never wanted to get anywhere close to that type of relationship ever again. I wanted to be sure I did not give up my freedom or risk being controlled again, or worse, abused. Plus, I didn't want to be a burden to him or anyone else, for that matter. Mick was okay with that. He didn't "allow me" or "forbid" me to do anything. Furthermore, I knew that people might see me or perceive me as a gold digger. I didn't necessarily concern myself with what other people thought about me, but I didn't want the people who knew us to think I was with Mick for money because I wasn't. I wanted to be with him and hoped he wanted to be with me. We had many things in common, but keeping our homes and our finances separate just felt like the right step in that direction.

Dating in general can be complicated. Dating with children in the picture can be so complicated times two. I couldn't go full steam ahead and not consider what a serious relationship with Mick could mean, good and bad, for my children. Therefore, I even asked the children at one point, "would you like a little bit of Mick or none at all." Their response was "we want a little of him." That was a great thing, as he could only handle the intensity of children and me for a short period of time as well, so it worked out for us all. We could retain our independence and come together when each of us wanted that to happen. It was not your traditional relationship, but at the time it really seemed okay to me. The truth is, I didn't even dare dream of a relationship where we shared everything. Coming from where I had been that was a much crazier dream than Faith Hill singing our song on The Oprah Show! The way I saw it, the odds were a lot better that my name was going to be on Faith's CD. I could not have articulated that to anyone, much less to myself, but it really seemed like Mick's need for an occasional lady in his life and my need for an occasional man in mine made us a good fit.

Late in the summer of 2004, Mick called; and with some urgency, asked me to meet him in town. The children and I had just finished up lunch, so I asked my neighbor to watch the children and I headed over to meet him. He told me he'd been looking for a safer neighborhood for us to live and he wanted us to move into the beautiful house I saw in front of me. My heart stopped. The house was absolutely beautiful. A rock path lead up the front steps to the door, two dormer windows, and a garage under the side room that was walled with windows. The yard was beautiful and I could imagine Hunter and Dorothy running and playing in the grass. I literally lost my breath as we looked at the house. The house had a beautiful white picket fence and represented all that a "home" means to most of us.

I hesitated to accept this generous offer, but finally agreed, but to certain terms. I told Mick how grateful I was but the deal was that I would continue to pay him what I was already paying for rent and utilities, and thanked him for making up the difference. I couldn't help but be excited.

When we first took the kids to the house, Mick made a big deal about the children going to "look for some goats." He had their absolute undivided attention. I could hardly contain myself and Mick was about to bust-a-gut, as well. We drove to a nearby park and walked up a giant hill as Mick and the kids went "looking for goats". Once we finally got up to the house, Mick kept on with the goat story and said that the owners told him the goats were in the back yard. Mick acted as though they had told him what to do and they all saw a swing and sat down. It was then that he rather casually mentioned that this was their new home. The looks on their faces that day is something I will never forget.

I know that a woman who lets the man she is dating move her into a nice home she cannot afford indicates a dependency I said I did not want. I worried that people would learn what I was doing and consider me Doc's "sugar baby", but I really cared for him and knew he did for me. Mick and I talked over all of my concerns. This move seemed like all of my dreams were coming true. It felt like a form of commitment from Mick and a chance for the kids to have a yard, and their own bedrooms! I decided to give it a try. I really felt I was making the best out of our circumstances. So the day before Halloween, we moved into our new home in downtown Gainesville. I was excited and nervous and had a mixture of confusing emotions, but I was so grateful for the beautiful new place to live.

The kids all pitched in to help me keep up the house and I was excited to have the responsibility of cutting the grass in the front yard. The smell of the grass fed my inner spirit and made me feel somewhat normal again.

Chapter 26 A new way

As I approached my one-year anniversary with the insurance company, I began assessing my financial situation more closely. Although I lived in a beautiful home, I still had no savings and no real way to provide in the event of an emergency. I simply had to find a way to make more money. My boss was a wonderful man, and I knew that he needed more of my time than I was able to give him and I still needed more time with my children. He had been so fair to me and kind to my children. He was a decent man and he'd given me opportunities when I needed them so desperately. However, I knew - even with all I had learned about insurance in the past year - it was in the best interest of the firm and my children for me to look for another job. My boss gave me plenty of time to look for new employment, and I was indebted to him for yet another act of random kindness.

After looking for many weeks, I took a job as a corporate sales rep for a gym in town. I jumped in, head first, and though I didn't necessarily realize it was on a trial basis, it was about the only job I had seen that remotely interested me or that I met the requirements. Fitness was my passion and I knew I could help corporations see the long-term benefit of keeping their employees healthy. I worked many long hours and was able to bring in many new clients, but I was still making less money than I had been at the insurance agency. I felt an old familiar panic.

One day, while I was at the gym, a man who'd heard a little of my story said that he had known girls who made very good money working in a gentleman's club. "You are in really good shape," he said. "And you seem to have a friendly personality, maybe you should consider it."

I literally had to pick my jaw off the floor. "I am 41 years old and have three children," I said to this virtual stranger. "Yes, but you seem to be in a need of more money and maybe you should just consider it," he replied.

I didn't know the man very well at all and actually never saw him again after that initial chance meeting; but that night, I lay in bed and thought about whether or not I could ever be in that line of work. I got up from my bed, walked over to my mirror, and started dancing like Demi Moore in Striptease and then laughed at myself. I ran back to my bed and crawled up under my covers and dismissed the idea completely. For the next few weeks, I kept plugging along at the gym, but the idea kept entering my mind. I felt like I had to do something to try to make more money, and my kids needed more time with me, as well. I absolutely was not going to crawl back to South Carolina and admit defeat. So one day, I pulled into a church parking lot of all places and made a few calls to some gentlemen's clubs that I had seen online. There, in the shadow of a steeple, I listened as the people on the other end of the line told me about the requirements to be a stripper. I didn't go to my Bible to look for guidance from God. I didn't pray for wisdom or seek Christian counseling. When you feel like you don't have any choices, those are the times your choices are most important. Instead, I began making appointments for interviews.

At the first club, I went just inside the front door and lost my nerve. The place just seemed tawdry, and I left without talking to anyone. "What are you thinking? You can't do this?" I told myself. I started to turn the car back to Gainesville, and then reminded myself that I was not going to be able to take care of my kids on what I was making at the last three jobs I'd held. I shook off the uneasy feelings I'd gotten at the first club and drove to the second place on my list. The manager at the second club met me at the front entrance and asked, "Have you ever danced for money before?" I answered with a resounding "no!" She smiled and nicely told me to come back when I had some experience. I drove home very disheartened. Are you kidding me? I am 41 years old. I don't have the luxury of time to get experience! And where would I get experience if no one would hire me? The infamous "Catch 22" playing in my mind all over again.

The last place on my list was The Cheetah of Atlanta. It was beautiful and just walking in, I was grateful I wasn't even considered for the other club. The staff was neatly dressed in coats and ties. This was my first real experience with a gentleman's club. I looked around at the lights, stage, and theatrical atmosphere. The place was full of beautiful women who were performing for the patrons. I was greeted at the door and introduced to the house mom on duty that night. She showed me around and we sat down to talk in private. As I expected, her first question to me was "have you danced for money before?" I had learned my lesson, and though it went against everything I believed in, I lied and responded with: "Why yes." I hated being dishonest and I am almost certain she didn't believe me, but I didn't know what else to do. She told me to get my permit and that I would start that Friday.

I knew that I had drawn a line way beyond where most people would draw it on that night. Most of us have nightmares about being naked in public and here I was asking for the chance to do just that! On the ride home from The Cheetah that first night, I was proud of myself. I kept thinking that this job would allow me to provide an income for my family so I wouldn't be a burden to anyone. I wouldn't need food stamps, Mick, my family, or anyone to provide for the kids. In addition, when my children needed me during the day, I'd be there.

Never in my life would I ever have imagined that I would actually be a stripper. I didn't much like the term "stripper" either and thought of myself more as an "exotic dancer" but I surely didn't think there was anything exotic about me. I remember standing off to myself in the club that first night and I prayed that God would not forsake me. I know that may sound like blasphemy to some, but only God knew my heart and He alone is the only one who can judge me. He knew I wasn't there for the thrill of it or to appease my wild side. I never even really had a "wild side." I wasn't even being greedy because I wanted a nicer car or jewelry or new luxuries. I simply needed a way to provide for my children. I had to know that if I were sick, I had a few weeks worth of savings that would see us through. Mick was active in mine and my children's lives, but we were not his responsibility and I needed to keep it that way for many reasons.

On the ride home, no worry or guilt filled my mind. I was grateful for the chance to earn more and have more time at home. I drove the long, dark straight strip of I-85 home in relative peace. Stripping was legal and gave me what I needed: more money and more time with my kids. I sincerely believed I wasn't hurting anyone and that if I didn't do it, someone else would. The idea that stripping was a "sin" didn't even enter my mind. Was that because God wasn't speaking to me? Perhaps it was just my selfishness: a desire to do things my way. I didn't see any way I could work two jobs and care for my children when all they needed was me there in person. Maybe I just thought it would feel good to have people be kind to me, to tell me I was beautiful, to be chosen. Maybe somewhere deep down inside me, I had begun to believe that all the things my husband had said about me were true: that I was worthless; and the only use anyone would have for me was my body. I cannot answer my critics and those who judge me, but I can say that I slept well that night and most nights after I began stripping.

Chapter 27 Charlie

My usual shift at the Cheetah started at 8 p.m. At home, I'd get in the tub at six each night, start getting ready then make the long drive to Atlanta. My permit was $350, but I made $250 the first night. That is a low night, but when I took the stage that first time, I was afraid I wouldn't even make a dollar so I was relieved! As hard as I had worked to keep my body in shape, I stood out primarily because of my age. In addition, I was lean muscle, so I really didn't have much to "shake." The club was full of beautiful young girls who quickly became dear friends to me. Many, like me, were working to provide for their children. Some were paying for their college courses. Before I became a dancer, I thought of all clubs as dirty and of the women as loose. Quickly, I learned that friends I had who wore suits to work each day had slept with more men than my friends who were dancers and took off their clothes for money. We all draw these invisible lines and say "that sin is worse that sin." I guess it makes us feel better to know we are not alone when it comes to goofing up.

I had a stage name, Charlie, to hide my real identity. I chose the name Charlie mainly because it reminded me of "Charlie's Angels." And let's face it, that was the era I came from. I was no spring chicken, by any stretch of the imagination, but I was surprised to find I could be myself even in an environment that was so foreign to me. The club I worked in was clean; and if a client tugged or pulled on a girl, they were quickly asked to leave. The Cheetah had no poles when I worked there and has a five-star restaurant. The clientele tends to be well-educated and successful career men. Of course, not all men go to strip clubs, but I saw all kinds of men at The Cheetah. Some were married and some even came in with their wives.

Each dancer at the Cheetah dances for a set of three songs and rotates every third set. I had learned the trade quickly: the importance of seduction, not to give away what you want them to pay to see. In many ways, dancing is brutal. Men choose you - or they don't - for a VIP room or table dance, all based on an immediate impression of you. It's like when the popular kids were picking kick ball teams on the playground in elementary school, only back then you were hoping they'd want you on their team. At the Cheetah, you were hoping they were willing to pay to see you naked or better yet, pay to just carry on a conversation with you in private. When you are not chosen, you cannot help but feel the rejection: "What's wrong with me? Why don't you like me? Please choose me."

Dancing can also be very good for the ego. When someone likes you, they say nice things, give you money, compliment you and make you feel valuable. There's also the very tangible value too: in the forms of tens, twenties, hundreds. I've read where another stripper said she felt "worshiped and violated all at the same time." Some men were jerks; most were very polite.

Occasionally when I was dancing in the club, I would look around the room and see the naked bodies gyrating behind or beside me and think "how in the world did I get here?" For the most part, I thought of stripping the way I thought of any other job. The men in the club were all aware of the nature of the business. Most did not come to the club looking for a relationship of any kind. They simply wanted to be entertained by beautiful women. And most of them knew and respected the fact that the women were there to make money.

Sometimes the pay was great. Sometimes I danced my heart out for mere gas money. Because I danced in a high-end club, I never felt threatened or in danger. The owners had set specific standards for acceptable behavior in the club. Dancers had to pass drug tests and breathalyzers in order to work and to leave each night. Bartenders helped make sure that when men were buying the dancers drinks that the dancers were not getting drunk.

When I hear horror stories from other strippers in clubs where drug and alcohol abuse were common as in "touching" clubs, I know that my experience as a dancer is very different from many other strippers.

After your song set ends, you put your clothes back on and go thank the people who tipped you. It was second nature to me to use the principles I had learned in my Mary Kay business: "Everyone has a sign around their neck that reads, "make me feel important." I made it a point to learn the names of the men who came to the club on a regular basis or who came in yearly for conferences in Atlanta. If I saw them back in the club at a later date, I'd call them by name and watch as their faces lit up because they were remembered. Being friendly, paying attention to the clientele and making them feel valuable is just as important for a good income to a dancer as having a good body and making the right moves. In my opinion, it's even more important. I didn't let the fact that I was a dancer, working for money, keep me from being human. I listened intently to the ones who wanted to spend time with me and I befriended every one of them. I saw them as real people and in return I made some life-long friends. It was never a "sexual thing" to me.

Some wives might have thought that I wanted to take their husbands, but if they had met me they would quickly learn that I was not that way. I can honestly say, I never wanted to take anything but an income and friendship from the relationships with the men I danced for. I believe the husbands who said they loved their wives and didn't want to be with anyone else. I was not there to steal anyone away from anyone. I simply did my job and tried to be the same, kind person I was to people I see in the grocery store every week. I was on a mission and didn't have time for folly. That being said, I hear the pain in the voices of women when they say that if their husband is lusting over a dancer, it is a kind of infidelity to her - that he's getting his needs met beyond their relationship. For the record, I, too, would be hurt if my husband frequented strip clubs or if my daughters were to become strippers so I can certainly understand. All I know is what I experienced and how I conducted myself while at the club.

When I was stripping, I thought of my dancing as entertainment, like a movie or a trip to the theatre. Occasionally, I also became a friend to some of the men I met in the Club. With that being said, I never led a client to believe it could be anything more. Thinking that way allowed me to justify what I did, I guess. I didn't see myself like that of the seductress in Proverbs because I didn't carry on relations with the men in or out of the Club.

The Club closes at 3 AM, so by a little after 4, I could be home. I'd catch a couple of hours or sleep and then get the kids up and off to school. I'd get another nap during the day then get up and exercise before the kids came home from school. I worked when they were sleeping. Working three nights a week I earned more than double to three times what I was earning working full time in my previous jobs.

For the first time since we had fled to Georgia, I was making the ends meet without anyone's assistance. I was able to buy a life insurance policy to provide for them if something happened to me and even saving some each month.

Chapter 28 Two very strong words

"Hate is a very strong word, Marian," my mother was saying. It was something she said all the time when I was growing up, and I knew she was right. At the time, I thought it might feel good to say such a "strong" word. I can't even remember why I was so angry. I was probably about six years old and pulling my homework from my book bag. I might have been angry with a teacher or someone who'd had been unkind to me at school. My mind flashed back to that memory of me at my mom's kitchen table as I sat with friends at one of Hunter's football games. A preschooler who was running around in the bleachers had used the word; and his mom - like my mom, like millions of moms around the world, and like I had always told my children, "Hate's a very strong word." I smiled at the child and the mother and found myself lost in thought. I wonder if we are wise enough to teach our children the same thing about the word love. We love chocolate and blame "falling in love" for all of our bad decisions. We're just not careful with a word that is the exact word God used to describe himself when He only wanted to use one word. Careless use of the word as it related to men has cost me. Truth is, it has cost me a lot more than misusing the word hate, but then again, I was taught not to misuse a word that was so destructive. I didn't know that misusing such a good word could be just as destructive. "My heart won out over my head," I'd say. Some men loved my style and demeanor at the club. My boyfriends had loved sex with me. If you do all the right things, people will say they love you. I have chased love and made love and then, all too late, I have realized that it wasn't love at all.

"Hate is a strong word, Marian." I learned that lesson well and don't even use it when I talk about my tormenter of ten years. Love is a very strong word, too, and I am learning to be more careful with it.

Chapter 29 A set back is a set up

I tried to be an excellent employee at The Cheetah. I arrived at work on time, did my best, and made it my goal never to cause a problem for my employer. During the first six months of employment, the Cheetah awarded me the "Role Model and Best Attitude Award". You may think "big deal," you got an award among strippers. Well, it was a big deal to me. I was doing a good job and the schedule allowed me to be involved with my children's activities during the day. While I was at the club I never missed a school field trip and that fact alone gave me great joy.

I relied on my brother, neighbors, varied sitters, and Mick to stay with the kids when I was dancing. Of course, Mick was the only person who actually knew what I was doing in Atlanta. He was supportive of my work at The Cheetah. Everyone else thought I was a showroom model. I loved being home with the kids and being able to go to their field trips and be home with them when they were sick without letting down my employer felt like a dream come true for me. However, I also felt extremely guilty for lying. I try very hard to be an honest person and having to alter every story I told about work and hiding my real feelings and experiences was exhausting. Mick was great to help out with the kids. He, like me, loved to stay in shape so he'd come over and we'd walk together, then he'd stay with the kids until I got home. It was a crazy schedule, but we made it work.

My reputation for being responsible made a difference at The Cheetah, and the management paid my $350 permit fee two years in a row to thank me for my excellent work ethic. I was never late. I always danced my stage set, and even helped out when they needed dancers at a moment's notice. I looked at my fellow workers as part of my team, or me a part of theirs and it felt good to help things go smoothly.

What I did was legal, and I kept telling myself that. But prostitution is legal in parts of Nevada. The fact that it's legal doesn't mean it's okay or good for the people who do it. If men paid me enough, I took my clothes off for money and danced. I wasn't doing ballet. I was dancing to entertain and please strangers. I've seen the statistics; and I know that the vast majority of strippers have been sexually abused at some point in their lives. The studies say that women who have been belittled and beaten down in their lives will do things that others would not because they desperately need the rewards offered by the patrons who find them attractive and beautiful. I suppose the sexual brutality and constant verbal abuse I endured in my second marriage makes me fit that stereotype. Would I have sold myself in this way, if I had never endured those empty nights in that little, concrete house? To this day, I cannot answer that question fully. Maybe in time I will be able to. I hope so.

I have learned that I have to fail forward to grow. And that a setback is always a setup for a comeback. It hurts me to think that anything I did perpetuated the idea that women are objects, the very kind of thinking that caused me such suffering in my life. I am grateful when people are able to suspend their need to put me down and condemn me for the decisions I have made. I know that the women I danced with and the staff of The Cheetah are some of the finest people I have ever known. Believe it or not, it helped me to have been in such good company.

Knowing strippers and being a stripper softened me in the same way I was softened as I walked into the DFACs office and the group sessions at The Gateway House. I am quicker to catch myself now when I start to judge someone for I have seen that by the same measure we judge someone, we will also be judged.

Chapter 30 Third time's a charm

I'd been dancing at the club for about a year when Mick told me that he was thinking of selling his business because he really wanted to move to the beach and simplify his life. I thought it best that the kids and I not be a hindrance to his dream, so we moved back into an apartment so that he could sell the house we had been living in. We were sad to leave the beautiful house with its big yard and white picket fence, but we packed everything up and moved across town into a small apartment.

The best advantage of the apartment was that there was a pool and lots of children for the kids to play with. For the first time in a long time, I could be with my children for breakfast and not have to rush off and leave them all day; and I had enough strength to really be there for them during the long days of summer. We'd be in the pool most of the day; and then at night we'd sit on the balcony of the apartment and watch the fireflies come out. It was not a traditional life. But we were together. We were family and it was good.

Mick's plan to sell the business didn't come to fruition, and eventually, Mick and I made plans to be married. We found a new house in a wonderful school district nearby. In the new house, the kids all had their own bedrooms. The girls were especially excited since they had shared a bedroom in the apartment for years. Just as he had before, Mick came up with a plan to surprise the children. He told them we needed to get a house ready for some new tenants. They all walked in and started looking around. Dorothy, who had decided when she entered first grade that she didn't want to be called Dodie anymore, walked into one bedroom and saw a big teddy bear sitting in the corner and instantly fell in love. Of course, it was in the room that was to be hers.

On the first day we were living in the new house we heard a horrible squealing noise coming from out back. In a minute, the children came rushing in to get me to help them. "What is it?" I asked, terrified that someone was hurt. "Hurry! It's trapped," they said. I was relieved and surprised to find a little goat trapped in a neighbor's fence instead of a child, but the poor little guy was in pain and scared to death. We pushed and pulled and finally got the little goat free. The kids started talking about the last house and how Mick had told them we were looking for goats there... but that this new house really had goats! Imagine that?

One of our new neighbors was an old friend to Dorothy. They had been playmates at day care for years. I was told by another one of our new neighbors from across the street that her daughter's first words had been my daughter's name. With the goats and the old friends, the new house became home to all of us almost in no time.

Because our wedding was to be the third for Mick and for me, as well, we decided to keep the ceremony simple. We hoped this one would be the "charm" for the both of us. Dorothy asked Mick if we would get married on her birthday, so we checked the calendar and decided on May 17th. We married at the side of the neighborhood pool on a beautiful, picture perfect day. I was wearing a gown Sydney had helped me select and we celebrated with a small gathering of friends and family. Mick had to attend some continuing education classes after our ceremony, so our honeymoon was to be at a seminar. Not the most romantic of destinations, but I was still filled with hope. Mick could give my children things I could not and he had very few requirements of me. It was such a welcomed change from the absolute domination I had lived under previously.

Our marriage was as non-traditional as our courtship had been. The kids and I continued to live in the house while Mick had a room in the new house, but mostly lived in the cottage beside his practice in town. I continued to work at the Club and provide for the kids and myself with the exception of the part of the mortgage which was above what I had been paying for rent. Of course, Mick was always very generous with gifts for the kids. At the time, my thinking was that we didn't have to follow anyone else's norms. It seemed to be working for the kids, for me, and for Mick. Many men have told me that they would not want their wives working in a strip club, but I was grateful at the time that Mick didn't tell me what I could or couldn't do. Mick knew I was there to make a living for my children and myself. I am sure he was also grateful for the financial help I offered to the relationship as I had always made that a priority for me. I liked the feeling of pulling my own weight. Shortly after we were married, another opportunity to move south came about and Mick and I went to check it out. It didn't come to pass, but the children and I had already moved back into town into an apartment complex and we decided to stay there due to location and convenience. The children and I loved the new complex and fit right in and made fast friends with our neighbors.

Of course, not living with your husband can be very lonely. I have never spent even a week with my husband where we fell asleep beside each other, woke up together each day, learned to change and re-adjust our habits to accommodate one another. Mick has never seen me without makeup and we've never had to sacrifice even half of a closet or space in a drawer to make room for one another in our lives. If I wasn't who he wanted me to be, or he wasn't who I wanted him to be, we could just go to our respective homes. No conflict. That was the idea. Nice in theory, but our arrangement required none of the normal give and take that most people know to be what strengthens a marriage, what makes each partner a better person, or what creates that sacred bond between a man and a woman. I didn't have to learn to be more patient or kinder and neither did Mick. I could continue to do things my way, and so could he. Eventually, we both began keeping a record of wrongs.

When I was working at the Cheetah, my coworkers knew I was married. Sometimes customers would ask me, and I was always honest: "yes, I'm married." My co-workers, from the bouncers to the other dancers, were good friends to me. Many of them were married, as well. Many of the girls had long-time boyfriends they'd met before they took their jobs at the Club. These were women who worked hard and respected one another. People who are judged as harshly as we are tend to be more accepting of one another. In spite of the very unusual place I was in my life: working at a strip club, married, but not living with my husband, I was making it and thanks to the people around me, I was learning a lot about myself.

Chapter 31 Facing my fears

Eventually, keeping a secret starts to take its toll on you. For all of the mistakes I have made in my life, I have never been a liar. I have been naive; I have taken "this" road when "that" road might have been best. I have failed in three marriages. I stayed with an abusive alcoholic, I have taken my clothes off for money, but I have never been a liar. Therefore, keeping the secret of my stripping was really hard for me and ultimately became unbearable. In 2008, Sydney and I were watching television together. Joy Behar was on The View. I remember looking over at Sydney and saying "it's time to write the book!" She looked at me and said "OK, mama, do it! I know you can do it!"

On the family chalkboard, which was just outside the entrance to my bedroom, I wrote in bold letters, "2008, This is our year!" I talked to Mick about writing "The Nineteen Cent Millionaire," and he sent me the sweetest email, saying he would buy me a laptop to help move the process along. I talked with my entire family about what the book would mean: people would know the truth. People would know that I was an exotic dancer and we might lose some friendships.

I began to experiment with telling strangers. When they asked me what I did for a living, I no longer lied. I told them flat out: "I am a dancer. I dance at The Cheetah in Atlanta." I was surprised by people's reactions. Maybe they were just being polite or trying not to be judgmental, but for the most part, everyone treated me with kindness. One woman caught me so off guard as she told me she'd thought about doing that for a while to make some extra money. Really, I thought to myself? Another moment where I had to pick my jaw off the floor? Case in point, we really don't know what people are thinking, do we?

Telling the truth became liberating, so I began writing, which became my own form of therapy. I would pour my memories on the page, then read my words days after. In the process, I began to see myself differently. I began to see how much of my life I had lived trying to make other people happy, to make someone like me. I did it when I danced and I did it when I lied about dancing. The lying made me feel worse about myself and I had to try to find the freedom to be open and to free myself and my children in the process.

Just two days after my husband had told me he was getting me a laptop so I could start on my book, I was getting my hair colored at my local salon. While I was waiting for the color to take, I took a phone call that happened to be from one of the day-time managers at the club. Holly was someone who made a great first impression that made her hard to forget. First of all, she was incredibly kind and friendly; and secondly, her last name was Wood; so her name was Holly Wood. Catchy, right?

"Charlie," she said, "a staff member from The Oprah Winfrey Show has just called, and they're looking for someone who breaks the stereotypical mold of a dancer to be on one of their shows." I couldn't believe what she was saying and began to think she might be joking. "This is for real, Charlie. They are doing an episode about what people are willing to do to make or save money; and we thought you would represent our club well."

I'd always loved The Oprah Winfrey Show and had watched it with Sydney when she was just a tiny little thing. Oprah always seemed like a person who empowered people and women especially. There was even a point in time, when I had little interaction with other adults and I began to look forward to 5 p.m. to see what good news Oprah could lend me. In particular, I remember one episode about strengthening your relationship with your mom that really helped me and my mother overcome some rough times. And too, I had been telling the children for years that we were going to be on The Oprah Show when Faith Hill sang our song. This wasn't exactly that dream, and I knew my decision could have a huge impact on my life and theirs. The more I thought about it, though, the calmer I felt about the whole thing. From the beginning, I thought how ironic it was that I had just made a decision to include my "stripping job" in my book and here I was getting an invitation to tell the world. I often wondered if I would have even considered doing the show had I not already made the call in my own mind to be open in my book. I was excited about the chance to meet Oprah, but that wasn't my focus. I was on a mission and I had a purpose. I couldn't shake the feeling that this was some detour in the waters for me and I saw their calling out of the clear blue sky as some kind of sign. I wasn't sure which way this would go, but I said "Sure, I'll talk with them." Within minutes, I was on the line with one of Oprah's team members. They told me they would be interviewing several people; and after they'd met me and the others, they would decide who they wanted to be on the show.

As exciting as it was to talk to the Oprah staff, I realized that being on national television talking about my job as a stripper was a huge step with major ramifications for me and my family. Shelly, my hairdresser, had finished with my hair. Women usually tell their hairdresser everything, but she knew nothing of my job as a stripper. It wasn't that I didn't trust Shelly, but I honestly thought she wouldn't love me anymore. I later told her about what was going on, and once again saw how wrong I had been to question her love for me. She was very supportive and encouraging and still is to this day.

I immediately went to my husband's office to tell him about the call I had just received. He seemed quite proud that the Cheetah had thought of me to be one of the girls to represent the club, and we decided we'd have to spend some serious time weighing the pros and cons before we made the decision to participate.

Each time the Oprah staff called, however, I learned a little more and felt more comfortable with the idea of sharing my story. They told me they were looking for a dancer who was older, preferably someone with a college education, or someone who'd run her own business in addition to being a dancer. They also hoped to find someone with children and to learn more about what prompts someone to become a stripper.

The Oprah team assured me that they would approach my segment in a positive manner. The professionals quickly put my fears to rest and treated me kindly in every encounter.

Mick and I talked with the kids about what I'd been offered. As best as I could, I told the kids that all of their friends would know what I did, and that some of them might not want to be their friends anymore. We discussed doing the show at length, weighing each of their thoughts, and afterwards, they told me it was my decision. I had never expected anything like this to happen and I remember not letting myself get overly excited as this wasn't my "dream plan" by any stretch of the imagination. My presence on Oprah would, at best, be considered "controversial" and my decision was not based on attention or any "15 minutes of fame." I saw it as an opportunity to rid myself and my family of guilt and shame and I just couldn't shake the immense coincidence of their calling. So I made my mind up that I would do the show if, indeed, they decided to call me back.

Many of the other dancers being considered for the segment declined the offer. They were not ready for everyone they knew to know how they earned their money. For some of the girls, being on Oprah could have cost them another job, or the support of their family. It was just too high a price to pay.

As for me, I was genuinely tired of worrying about what people would say and what they'd think of me based on my occupation. I had made my decision to come out in my book, so my mind was mentally ready for this undertaking. I thought it was better for me to come out, to be honest, and actually tell the truth rather than hide behind this façade any longer. Timing is key in everything we do in life. I didn't leave my captor after the first time he hit me, and it had taken me three years to get comfortable coming out with my story. We each grow in different ways and in different measures of time. That's what makes us all unique. I wanted to positively represent myself and the other women like me who made a choice to become strippers to provide for their families. I could not change everyone's preconceived notion of what kind of person a stripper is; but maybe I could help people see the women who are exotic dancers as real people with real dreams and real fears.

Once the Oprah team had decided to have me on the show, we scheduled a time for them to come to our apartment and film us living out a normal day. They scheduled a day when they could follow me around all day with the kids then as I went to work to show how I went from being a regular mom to a stripper.

In the days before the team arrived, I received a call from the club's manager, Jack. He wanted to make sure that I was okay with doing the show. "Don't feel any pressure from us, Marian. It will be good publicity for the club, no matter what, but it could be rough on you." He wanted to be sure I didn't feel pressure to do anything and that it was going to be okay with my family. He even warned me of the possibility that it could go very badly, due to public opinion. He was looking out for my well-being. I cannot tell you how much I appreciated his call. It proved to me, once again, that he cared more about me more than the publicity for the club. But if I did do the show, I wanted to do a good job for him and for everyone else. They had become like family to me and I wanted to make them proud. I wanted to stand up for my friends.

Lisa Ling, a correspondent with the Oprah show who had been a host on The View, was set to come to our apartment with the camera crews first thing one Friday morning. Mick called from his house the night before they got there to wish me well and check on me. I was nervous and excited and slept very little that night. At 6 AM, the crew arrived at the front door of our apartment. The crew gave me the very difficult task of acting like they weren't even there as I got the kids up, fed, and off to school. They were wonderful and well-behaved, which is basically the norm for our house, but as most parents know, mornings can be one of the most hectic times for a family. But my children are troopers and they knew this was important. The camera crews followed them out to the school bus which, of course, they all thought was pretty cool.

The crew told me to do whatever I would normally do and they'd film me. I told them it was a good thing I hadn't worked the night before or they'd have several hours of watching me sleep. Instead, I had my fiber cereal, drank some coffee and hit the Stairmaster. I felt odd as they filmed me, but their personalities made it easier to relax. I showed them around the apartment to let them get a glimpse of what our family was really all about. Our refrigerator was covered with the decorations of most proud families: photos, artwork, graded tests and homework assignments with big red "A"s. Lisa Ling and I talked for most of the morning as she gathered background information about me and how I'd become a stripper.

It just so happened to be an early release day for the schools, so by mid-afternoon, the children were home, riding their bikes and playing around the apartment complex. Lisa asked Sydney if she'd be willing to talk with her in an interview, and Sydney willingly agreed as did I. When I saw the interview sitting right next to Oprah, I teared up as I watched my 13-year-old confidently speak to Lisa Ling as the cameras rolled. She was so beautiful. Her hair was softly pulled just off her face and occasionally the wind would lift a wisp of hair as she told Lisa and the world what life was like with me for a mom. She told Lisa she was proud of me and my heart melted. Neither of us had any idea she would be interviewed, but Sydney conducted herself with such grace and maturity. I had taken her away from everyone she had ever loved and everything she knew when she was only seven, so she had grown up fast. She had handled all of the crazy things life had thrown at her so well and it had given her a beautiful inner strength. I am sure I relied too much on Sydney for emotional support as she grew up. I was such a mess when we first fled from South Carolina to Georgia. I am so grateful for the strength of Sydney's spirit and her unwavering love for me.

After all the interviews were complete, the camera crews came in and filmed me as I cooked dinner. I was so nervous I burned the first batch of meat for the tacos. "Great!" I thought out loud. "Now everyone will think strippers can't even cook tacos. I was a world-class chef in the making, no doubt!" I tried not to think about the fact that I was being filmed by camera crews for a national television show that was, indeed, about to film me as I worked as a stripper. So with no pressure at all, I tried to focus on the job at hand which was my next batch of taco meat.

After dinner, we headed off to the club where they were to film my co-workers and myself. I was especially nervous about this part of the interview; but the crew was nice and helped me feel at ease. We walked in to The Cheetah and I introduced them to several people and showed them around the club. I always did my own hair and makeup to save money, but for the show that night, the crew filmed as I became "Charlie." I was not used to all the fuss over me and it actually made me quite uneasy.

Looking good is very important to the income of a stripper. Makeup artists added hair extensions and false eyelashes to help me look my best. Cameras rolling: my entire life had become an open book to the crew that had spent the entire day with me. I felt like they were part of my family and it was odd to think of dancing for people who felt like my brothers and sisters. I imagine they felt the same way about filming me dance. One of the producers had taken a special liking to Dorothy and said he would just pack her up in his suitcase. I believe even they could see the normalcy in our family even through the dysfunction of our situation.

The club was hopping by the time we got there and the managers had their hands full with all the legal procedures in preparation for the show. In fact, everyone who worked at the club, from the makeup artists, to the bartenders, to the floor men, etc. all had to sign a waiver in the event they were seen on the show. There were many girls who didn't mind having their faces on television, but there were many more girls who simply couldn't risk it due to the stigma placed on someone who works at this type of club. It could have hurt their family members or other employers. I made a point to show the Oprah staff just how many of the girls didn't participate in the program to show how concerned these girls were with their reputations and how they had to hide. And all to avoid people's preconceived ideas and judgments.

For some of the girls, like me, they felt they had to be untruthful with family members, coworkers at other jobs, and other bosses because working at a strip club could get them fired or worse. But dancing for a living didn't mean these girls were loose or that they were bad people. In fact, some of them were as straight-laced as they come. They worked hard and I cared about each and every one of them.

The girls who were in my walkout for the evening had all signed consent forms, so we donned our evening gowns and took the stage together. It was an emotional walk out for me, knowing the cameras were rolling. In a matter of minutes, I would be filmed before national television as I stripped off my clothes and took money from men. I was scared to death, but I steadied myself on my heels and began dancing. I felt more vulnerable than I ever had before. I knew they would not be able to show me to the world the way the men in the club saw me, but there's something different about being a stripper to a select group who only know you as Charlie, and being Marian Wardlaw Shannon a "stripper-mom" to everyone who bothered to tune in to one of the most watched television show in the world.

I tried to forget the cameras were there and just continued to do my job. When it was over, I was glad it was behind me. After we finished and when it was time for me to go back home, I asked the crew why we had to have any semi-nude scenes at all. Couldn't they just show us walking into the Cheetah, kind of like using an ellipse in a story, "dot, dot, dot?" "We've told people I am a stripper, so they know what that means." I really didn't think they would go for that, but I guess I had to try. I didn't necessarily like it, but I knew that footage would have to be in the segment.

For the record, I was not ashamed of what I did for a living, but my job was always done in a setting where there were no children present. I knew my older children would be watching the show and that fact made me uncomfortable. I had lied to my children when I had first taken this job. Later on, I had told the two oldest what I really did for a living and tried to answer all of their questions. My children are all good students, good athletes, kind, caring, and loving individuals. They are not perfect, but they are remarkably close to it. They have lived through a lot, and it has made their hearts pliable and their minds open. Being honest about my job was tough at first, but I wanted my children to be honest with me so how could I ask that of them if I couldn't also be honest with them in return? I wanted them to know that whatever they went through in life, they could always come to me to talk about it. Through it all, my children have been strong, caring, and wonderful. We have grown closer as we've gone through our lives together. They know how much I love them and that I would do anything to take care of them.

As I drove home that night, I was extremely tired from a long day of talking and sharing my life with the camera crew, but I was pleased it had gone so well. I also felt like I had made some new friends that day. I told them during the interview that dancing/entertaining was what I did for a living at the present time, but it was not what defined me as a person. I could still be myself whether I was at the grocery store or dancing in the bright lights. I didn't even know for certain whether or not Oprah would want me to be on her show. Everything we shot that day could have ended up never being used. I was okay with that too, though I did hope I would have the opportunity to be on the show.

My three years at the Cheetah had helped me become more tolerant and taught me to go easy on people before making a snap judgment. I didn't make as much money every night as some of the younger dancers, but the money was more than I had ever made before. It allowed me to begin a small savings account. It took away some of the pressure I felt every month as I tried to pull the ends together and meet a very small budget. It gave me flexibility to be with my children, and brought with it some great, life-long friends.

As I was driving to work the next night, I got a call from the people at HARPO, saying I was going to be on the show. I immediately called my husband and told him the news. They would fly two of us to Chicago, so there was no question as to who deserved to go. I thought it would be a great experience for Sydney and she deserved the trip most definitely!

We had a lot to do to get ready: The HARPO legal team was very thorough. I had to send them my divorce records, employment history, support for everything I had told them. It was going to be a fast 24 hours, so the two of us made out our wish list and schedule. Sydney was so excited because she got to miss school, and she had only flown once before, so she was doubly thrilled. Sydney was a great traveling companion. I took along some yarn and had Oprah's scarf ready before we even got on the plane. It was the color purple. Ha, go figure! The experience of an airport has always been so fun to me. I love to people watch and try to imagine where everyone is going or where they've been. It's exciting to think of going somewhere new. Sydney and I were ecstatic.

When we arrived at the Chicago airport, a fellow traveler on the plane came up to tell me that he and his family had enjoyed watching us talk and giggle during the flight. He said they got a kick out of how much fun we were having just because we were on a plane, headed to Chicago. It was a big deal for us, and we had a blast together.

We felt like celebrities as we walked through the airport terminal and were greeted by a chauffeur standing with a sign that had our names on it. It's never taken much to excite me and so I asked Sydney to take a picture of me with the chauffeur. If I'm not mistaken, her name was Shirley and she was precious! I'm quite sure we looked like "rookies," which we were; but we were enjoying every minute and didn't want to pretend otherwise. Sydney quickly made herself comfortable in the limo. It was great to see her having such a good time. The driver was so kind and took us on a mini-tour of the city. She pointed out the designer stores and all the city landmarks.

Our driver also took us by Harpo Studios, and we were able to see the crew that had come to visit us in Georgia. We also got to meet the director, and a few more friendly faces, as well. Then we were taken to the hotel where we were to stay on the 25th floor of the Omni. We put our things away in the beautiful room and I went to check out the pool and weight room. Those of you who know me can all say, "of course" together! I knew I would need to work out at some point to loosen up from the plane ride and more importantly, to de-stress before the next morning. Sydney and I also needed to get our nails done and we were fortunate to find a great shop that was right in line with what we paid when we treated ourselves back home. Sydney wanted to show me all the designer stores so we did that, too. We walked around the streets of Chicago marveling at all the beautiful stores and merchandise therein.

Mick had given Sydney some money to spend while she was in Chicago; and needless to say, it was burning a hole in her pocket. She rewarded herself with her very first pair of Coach shoes and a Coach bag to match. She even began to tell the salespeople that I was going to be on The Oprah Show the next day. I was still a little timid to just come right out and tell them why, but I was slowly getting used to the idea. To my surprise, people were always very polite when I was honest with them. Next, we hit what we were told was Oprah's favorite store, the popcorn store. We had heard she mixes the caramel corn with the cheese popcorn or something like that. We decided to play it safe and Sydney went for the buttered popcorn and I enjoyed some caramel corn. Mmmmmm, it was delicious! Back at the hotel, I got in some cardio and weights while Sydney played in the pool. It was during my work out that I had a coincidental meeting with another patron of the hotel who just happened to know a guy I had been great friends with at Clemson. What a gift, to see someone who knew an old friend in such a big city. It's a small world, indeed.

After our workout, we headed back up to the room and ordered room service and relaxed together. We both worked on some scarves we were making for our friends at HARPO. We talked and had a great time together. During the evening, the staff from HARPO called several times and asked a few more questions; but on the whole, it was a very peaceful night. Well, as peaceful as it could be when I knew I was going to meet Oprah, be on national television, and be shown in a censored segment as I stripped at the Cheetah. Yeah, right. No pressure!

So remembering the words of my dad, "Don't get nervous, Marian, just because this is the most important race of your life," I calmed myself down and tried to prepare myself for the next day. Ever since I had started at the club, I would say "I'll sleep when I'm dead." I didn't sleep much that night, but it was enough and I awoke feeling confident and rested.

Chapter 32 A "single" statement

When the alarm went off, I prepared a nice hot bath and began getting ready for a very important day in my life and the lives of my children. I had laid out my clothes the night before and I just tried to gather my thoughts as I got ready. I ate a little breakfast to try to soothe my stomach, gave Sydney a big hug, and told her I loved her. Then I headed downstairs to meet the limo for the ride to the studio. Sydney was not allowed to go to the show due to the adult nature of the show, so she slept in and enjoyed room service, compliments of Oprah. We met back up for lunch after the show had been taped.

When I arrived at the studio that morning, I could feel myself getting very nervous. I tried to take a lot of deep breaths and use my swimming experience to maintain my composure. One of my coaches used to call me "Nervous Nellie," but I had been in many nerve-wracking situations in my life, so I knew I could do this. The staff and crew at HARPO were incredible. They helped me with my hair, did my make up; and though I wanted more eye makeup, I went with the flow. I also took one of my scarves that I was finishing up to keep me occupied while I waited. So there I was, crocheting in the green room, waiting to go on national TV. As I waited for my turn to meet Oprah, I was surprised to learn that the green room wasn't green at all. Hmmmm, I thought that to be pretty odd, but interesting at the same time.

As the moments progressed, a stream of different people came in to talk with me. Some needed to ask me questions, others helping me with this or that. I was growing more and more nervous, but the people who came in and out of the room help to calm my nerves.

Then the show began. I was not in the first segment, so I was able to watch the show progress from the no-so-green, green room. When the time came for me to go on, I walked through a little room to get on the actual stage and much to my surprise, all of the crew who had worked on the show were all sitting there, side by side, watching from their respective perches. I gave them all a "thumbs up" signal and said, "Let's do this!" They all smiled and wished me well.

I walked around the corner and onto the stage and saw Oprah sitting there. How many episodes of Oprah had I watched from my little home in South Carolina? How many shows had I watched at home in Georgia? Too many to count and here I was about to be face-to-face with an American icon: a TV legend and someone I greatly admired. She was looking at me and I was wondering whether she would like me or not. I was relieved to find she was sweet from the very beginning and it helped me feel more at ease. The time had come and there was no turning back now.

During the clip, Oprah began to read off a teleprompter. I heard, or at least I thought I heard, through the thunderous pounding of my heart deep in my chest, that she said I was a single mom. At the first available break, I leaned over to the lady who had interviewed me and said, "I thought I told you guys I was married?" She nodded, but told me they thought it was too confusing to explain to the viewers that I was a single mom when I turned to this profession, had married in the last 7 months, but didn't actually live with my husband. I took a deep breath, and said, "Ok, I see your point," but that didn't keep me from freaking out right there on stage.

I turned back toward the audience feeling absolute confusion. I had come all this way to get the truth out, and this was something I had not anticipated at all. Not in my wildest dreams. Here I was sitting with Oprah Winfrey on national television. I had no idea what she thought of me. I didn't even know if she knew that I had gotten married during the last year of my dancing or not. I surely didn't want to lose my composure so soon in the show, but I didn't want to appear deceitful either. I didn't want to create a problem in the show or get someone in trouble for having messed up. I had been told by one staff member that Oprah likes to come into each show basically like an audience member, fresh and hearing the information for the first time. I didn't know if Oprah knew that I was married, but I knew hundreds of people in my life knew. I didn't want to be seen as deceiving anyone because I had been totally honest about everything.

When the crew had come to Gainesville, I had asked Mick if he wanted to be involved in the filming. It happened to be his busiest day of the week and he had said "This is about you." Never had I deceived anyone at HARPO about my marital status.

With only a few seconds to deliberate, I decided I would wait to see if she asked me about my husband or being married later in the show, and if she didn't, I would talk to them immediately after the show. I was wearing my wedding ring, and all of the audience and viewers could easily see it. All I could think to do under that much stress and with so little time to mull it over, I decided to go with the flow of her questions and pray I'd have the opportunity to clear things up before the show aired.

Later, they told me that they had made a decision to list me as single, based on what I had told them about how I lived and what they had observed. In fact, I was living in the apartment with the kids while my husband lived across town. I paid my apartment rent of $1000 a month, did not have a joint checking account or credit card with Mick's name on it, nor did he share the day-in-day-out responsibilities of raising the kids with me. "What we saw was a single mom," he had said. That phrase kept replaying in my mind. Plus, we wanted to know what lead you to a career as a dancer, not necessarily where you were right now.

"But I'm married," I said out loud again. This was bugging me in a way that was out of proportion with the error.

After many years have passed now, I didn't then and still don't believe there was any conspiracy to be fraudulent on the part of the producers of the show. The purpose of the program was to tell the story accurately and concisely. The truth was my marriage would have been a topic for a completely different show! They were simply reporting on why I had made the decision to begin dancing in the first place and I had, indeed, been single when I became a stripper. In hindsight, I think they could have just left out the word "single" and still told the story, but it was what it was.

The use of the word probably didn't matter to anyone but me, my family, and those who knew me from Gainesville. But regardless, those were and are the most important people in the world to me, and I didn't like the idea that people might think I had been untruthful.

I tried to keep my mind focused on what was happening as Oprah began to ask me questions. The first segment that came on was Lisa Ling's interview with Sydney. It literally brought me to tears. She did such a wonderful job. She was so brave and poised. Oprah even sighed when she watched the clip of Sydney. Oprah was worried that her friends would see the show and lower their opinion of Sydney. She said she was concerned that parents of her friends would not want their children to play with

Sydney. I nodded, knowing that people do judge and that we all want to protect our children. But I also knew Sydney's friends and their loyalty to her. Sydney is a remarkable young lady and her friends know that about her.

After they showed the segment of me dancing in the club, Oprah commented on my abs. I was flattered and told her if I had not been in shape I never would have even considered dancing. I was in financial trouble and had to do something quick. Because I was in shape, stripping became an option I felt physically prepared for. I merely answered the door when opportunity came knocking.

The topic of the show was "Living on the Edge: How Far Would You Go?" Other guests, like me, had made lifestyle choices that are also considered outside the norm for society. One had left a six figure job to "dumpster dive" for food because she was offended by the consumerism of our culture. She basically lived on food that other people threw away... most of it unopened and still in its original packaging. Strippers and "freegans" don't follow society's rules and are willing to deal with the consequences of stepping outside those norms. I am sure there was some judgment between the guests when we first met: perhaps they thought of stripping as immoral and "diving" as a moral decision to avoid waste. I admit I was put off by the idea of eating anything someone had thrown away. But I'm as frugal as they come and as I listened to the other guests and got to know them, I was surprised at how much I could care and respect them. I hoped the same was true in reverse.

Only one person from the audience asked me a question, which Oprah herself answered for me. I felt as though Oprah liked me and I was grateful for her kind spirit. She posed for a photograph with me and I walked to the back of the studio.

Everyone who'd worked on the show was behind the set and they all encouraged me and thanked me. I was glad to hear that they thought it went well, but I needed to see the producer. I kept hearing Oprah say "single mom" in my mind, and it bothered me. The producer explained their reasoning, which I respected, but just didn't want to hear. "What we saw when we filmed... was a single mom."

"But this will confuse people who know me," I said. On a very deep level of my heart, it confused me too. I had made so many excuses and justifications for the decisions I had made. It wasn't Mick's fault. He was very clear about what he wanted. I merely went along with it. My fears of being controlled or abused by another man had made me afraid of what most people call marriage: really sharing yourself, sharing your life. It wasn't Mick's fault.

The producer promised he would take it to the higher-ups and have them make the decision about my segment before it aired.

I had done what I could and I was glad it was over. I had done it. I had told everyone my secret. I felt victorious if for no other reason that I faced my fears and went at them with my head held high. The limo took me back to Sydney and we had lunch with the other guests of the show. We took some photos together and had a great time conversing with them.

Then, as I had promised Sydney, we went on a long walk through the downtown area. It was freezing cold, and occasionally a snow flurry dropped from the clouds above the Windy City. The city was bustling with cars, noise, and people everywhere. It was very different from our little town, but the people smiled at these Georgia girls wrapped tightly in our big coats. As we walked, I replayed the show in my mind. I began to wonder if I had done the right thing by agreeing to be on the show. I wondered if I had said the right things. Did I represent the girls and the club well? Would my being on the show hurt my precious children? I didn't want to ruin my short time in Chicago with Sydney with my worrying, so I called the producers and discussed a few more things, as I knew they hadn't closed down the show just yet. I felt better after my conversation with them and I turned my attention back to my short time with Sydney.

We had a flight to catch and some food vouchers still unused, so being the ever frugal mom, I took Sydney to the restaurant to warm up and got our food packed to go. The driver came, picked us up, and we asked if we could go by The Harpo Studios one more time before we headed to the airport. He graciously agreed. Sydney and I had finished the scarves to give to our new friends, and we just wanted to say good bye one last time. While we were there, one of the producers came out and began talking with Sydney and told her how impressed Oprah had been with her. This made Sydney feel very special. She had such high hopes to meet Oprah, but didn't get the chance. The producers told her "maybe next time." That made Sydney very happy.

As the limo driver took us to the airport, we both agreed we could get used to the kind treatment we had been given on our whirlwind trip to Chicago. We had received Oprah t-shirts, mugs and hats from the staff. By the time we got to the airport, Sydney had already put on her shirt. People immediately started asking if we had gone to the show. Sydney, without any hesitation, began to tell everyone that her mom had been one of the featured guests. Of course, they then all began to ask what the story was about, and she told them without any hesitation. She was confident and proud of herself and of me it appeared. I knew she was going to be fine now. No more secrets. No more hiding. That, in and of itself, was very liberating for the both of us.

On the plane, I smiled at Sydney. We reached for each other's hands and sat back in our seats to enjoy the ride home.

When we arrived in Atlanta, Ricky, a longtime friend of my husband, came to pick us up. Mick was at the apartment with Hunter and Dorothy and had stayed with them while we were in Chicago. We'd only been gone for 24 hours, but we hugged on each other as if we'd been apart for weeks. I slept in the next day, which was a Friday. The last two weeks had been so emotional for me. The show wouldn't air until the following Wednesday and that added to my stress. I was glad for the tape delay though, because I still hadn't told my mother or brother the truth about how I had made my living and I had promised Oprah I would.

I worked at the club that Saturday and Monday and on Monday afternoon my brother called me and said, "Are you going to be on Oprah? We saw a promo for one of this week's shows." I said, hesitantly, "well, that's what I was about to come talk to ya'll about." As it turned out, they had known for quite some time that I had been working at the club, but never told me that they knew. I had worried myself sick wondering if they would still love me if they knew what I was doing. I apologized for not being forthcoming with them and they accepted my apology. My brother and his wife were very gracious and wondered why I had been so afraid to tell them.

Early Wednesday morning I got the kids off to school and drove to Clemson to confront my mom and tell her the truth. On the ride up, I received a call from an Atlanta radio station asking if I would be willing to be interviewed on air the day after the Oprah Show was broadcast. I agreed and then spent the rest of the ride trying to imagine how my mom would react. Would she cry? Would she be angry with me? Would she be disappointed? As it was, Mom and I talked for over three hours. I told her everything. I told her my fears and about the Oprah show. Mom was very understanding. She knew, probably better than most people in my life, what I had been through and my financial situation. I believe it was one of the best talks my mom and I have ever had. It warmed my heart that she could still love me so much. As a mom, I completely understand that kind of love. And I am happy to say that our relationship has grown closer and stronger since the show aired. Mom and I said our good byes and I headed back to Georgia to be home with the kids when the show aired. I knew there would be censored segments of me dancing in the club and I worried about that for them. When the show started, I held my breath as I heard the phrase again "single mom." I told myself they used that word because they reported how I had gotten into that line of work. That was their focus. I tried to forget hearing them say "what we saw was as single mom."

When the segment ended, I asked the children what they thought and tried to listen closely to what they said. They all seemed to think it went well and told me how much they loved me. I honestly believe they were most proud that I had the guts to face my fears head on and could still hold my head up high. I asked them if they thought people would be mean to them at school, but none of them seemed the least bit worried about the fallout for themselves.

I had to work that night, so when the show finished, I got in the tub, got the kids tended to and drove to Atlanta. During the drive down, several people called to tell me they had seen the show. Of course, my friends were very gracious and positive. When I walked in at the Cheetah, everyone was abuzz and pleased with how the show had gone. Several of the girls thanked me for stepping out of my comfort zone to represent them and myself. One girl even told me, after seeing the show, that she talked with her mother for the first time in years and they were on the mend. My heart was overcome by those kind of comments.

I had hoped that by being on the show, I could help dispel some of the preconceived ideas most people have about strippers. I hoped they would see that people who dance for a living are just that: people. When you take away a person's humanity, you're basically saying they are worth less than you are. If a stripper is not a person, she is beyond redemption.

I would never be foolish enough to think that a brief segment on a talk show could change whether or not someone thinks stripping is wrong. I respect the opinions of people who say stripping evokes lust and an unrealistic view of intimacy in sexuality. Oprah isn't the only talk show that had a mom/stripper as a guest. There's a long list of shows that have done similar segments. Playboy has had interviews with many other stripper moms. Other people were out there, telling their stories. I simply told mine. All I could do now was hope to show a real person who had decided to be in that line of work as she dealt with real life. I had never asked to be anyone's hero, yet I didn't feel I deserved to be condemned by anyone either.

At the club that night, they wanted me to walk out last again because that's what I had done when they were taping for the show. I was running on very little sleep and everything took on a surreal, dreamlike quality. As I made my way out on the stage, Jack, our General Manager, and Bob, our Owner, met me in the middle of the stage and offered their thanks in front of the whole crowd. I was so flattered by the kind words and was a tad overcome with emotion by that point. My eyes welled up with tears. It had been such an emotional rollercoaster for the past few weeks, but it was wonderful to be in the presence of friends and to feel appreciated. It really was a wonderful night at the club. I thought about how much everyone needs to feel appreciated and valued.

When I arrived home a little after 4 AM, I climbed into bed and fell into a much-needed, long-awaited, deep sleep.

My dream world didn't last long as the alarm buzzed at six. I pulled myself from beneath the covers and got the kids off to school.

Chapter 33 Reaction and reality

After the kids were off, I received the telephone call from the Atlanta radio station as promised. While on the air, someone called in and mentioned that I had been referred to as a single mom and had been dishonest. I tried to explain what had happened and that I had never lied to the team at Oprah. I had been afraid that their decision to say that I was single would cause this type of added controversy and it seemed to be true. Maybe I should have been angry with the HARPO staff, but I wasn't. I wished that they had not mentioned my marital status at all, but I understood their viewpoint. I know what they saw when they came to film us.

People who knew us were infuriated because they thought I had lied to Oprah so that I would fit her story profile. One blogger said I did it because I'd do "anything for my 15 minutes of fame." Even though I knew the truth, those type of comments hurt me deeply. I had just admitted to the world that I took my clothes off for money, why would I lie about being married? The cruelty of some of the callers and bloggers was a real surprise to me. I think maybe, they thought Mick was taking care of all of the bills and I stripped because of some form of sexual perversion on my part. I racked my brain trying to figure out what would cause them to become so upset about Oprah's staff's decision to say I was single.

I later told a friend, "I was ready to be ridiculed for being a stripper. That's fine. I did that. I was not prepared, however, to be called a liar when I had never lied to the Oprah team."

The bashing got so bad in the weeks that followed that my husband suggested I take some time off from work. He later suggested that I quit altogether, so that's what I did. I didn't like feeling as if I were being pushed out of something that provided a living for my family, but being on the

Oprah show had stirred up lots of emotions for me. Among them, a desire to become certified as a personal trainer, so instead of viewing this turmoil as a dead end street, I tried to view it as my golden opportunity. If my appearance on Oprah had closed one door, I knew it had to open another. I was ready for a new path.

As I began my training, I kept obsessing about the fact that people thought I had lied. I contacted the producers at Oprah and told them about the cruel things people had said to me or my husband about the fact that I was introduced as a "single mom." I asked that they please send me something in writing that acknowledged that I had not misrepresented my life in anyway, that I had been honest about my marriage to Mick, as abnormal as it was. Much to my surprise, they did not hesitate and within two minutes, they sent me an email stating that they knew I was married and that I had not misrepresented myself in any way and it was their decision to call me a "single mom." The team was equally surprised that the story had generated such a response. I copied the email and carried it with me everywhere I went. I felt like I had to defend myself. It was almost funny! I didn't have to defend myself for taking my clothes off so men would tuck bills in my garter, but I had to carry around a little email like a mini shield to prove to people that I didn't lie about being married.

Long after the rubble started to settle, I was still troubled by the whole thing. When we look at ourselves, we can only see life from the vantage point of our eye sockets. It's a limited viewpoint with a kind of tunnel vision. Sometimes, we can see ourselves more fully, like in a mirror. The Oprah show was a kind of mirror for me in many ways. It showed me a very determined woman who was willing to risk the possible criticism of family and friends to finally tell the truth through a unique opportunity. It also showed me some things about myself I didn't necessarily like. "What we saw was a single mom."

I had tried to pretend that my arrangement with Mick was a functioning marriage; and in some ways, I guess it was. I had to admit to myself that in many ways, I had kept Mick at a distance, just like I did the men in the club. Of course, he was my husband, and that analogy can only go so far, but the boundaries we had set up prevented us from really knowing one another and making the hard changes that are necessary for two people to be genuinely intimate with one another on the level God intended for husband and wife. For someone who has spent a lot of time trying to make sure I liked what I saw when I looked at a mirror, I didn't like some of the things I was beginning to see. I couldn't really be mad at Mick. He had told me he didn't want to be a traditional husband and father from the get go. Our arrangement worked for him. As much as he didn't think he was ready or capable to be the best dad for my children, he did love them and do many wonderful things for them. I had really thought it would work for me, as well, but it left me with a deep longing. I was technically married, but as I rolled over in my bed at night, the bed was empty. If I had time to even allow myself to think about what I was feeling, I was profoundly lonely. With what I had been through, I had to wonder if I was going to ever be able to trust anyone enough to open my heart and my home. Plus I had a deep ache that made me ask myself, "What am I teaching my children about marriage? Is this really how I want them to live?"

Mick and I talked and decided that it was time we gave living together a try. I was so hopeful, yet terribly nervous. My last experience with that had imprisoned me, and though I knew Mick was not at all like my previous husband, he had always told me traditional marriage wasn't his plan. This was a big risk and we both knew it. So for the first time into our married life, we actually moved in together as a family in one house: husband, wife, children and Tigger the cat.

Over a weekend, we all moved in to the house we had lived in before our last stay in the apartment. Mick had already lived there before, as well, while repairs were being made on the cottage beside his office. The repairs had long been completed so if he ever needed a get-away, his cottage was an option for him. But our plan was to try to care for, respect, and honor each other under one roof.

Because I was breaking the lease, the apartment complex asked for the $2000 contract penalty for first and last month's rent. Mick offered to pay it, but I was tormented that I was taking his money. It was the first time I had ever needed money for living expenses from him. I cried as fear got the best of me and I thought "I'm back to square one." A dear friend whom I lovingly call "my ex-wife-in-law" was a great comfort to me at that time. She had been married to the father of my children before he and I met. She and I have always been good friends. "Honey, Mick is your husband," she said to me. "Husbands and wives share things, help each other out like that. Most marriages have joint everything. It doesn't mean he's controlling you. It doesn't mean you can't support yourself. It means you're partners. It's a give and take."

Her words were sweet and gentle and I really wanted to believe them. The truth is it sounded like a fairy tale to me. I could not imagine a time when I would ever know that kind of relationship. At the club, every monetary encounter was such an obvious exchange: "I did this. I got that." There's a certain assurance to the clarity of the transaction. Marriage, where the give and take is so transient was hard for me to grasp. I thanked her for her words of wisdom, clicked the end button on my cell phone and tried to smooth over my make up to cover the paths that the tears had cleared down my face.

I know that if the situation were reversed, I wouldn't have hesitated to help Mick. But I could not imagine a marriage where you really share everything: bank accounts, responsibilities, child rearing, a bed every night, life. I wasn't sure if Mick could do it. I wasn't sure he wanted to. I was even afraid that after all this time, I couldn't.

The next month was hard on my ego. From the first time after I got on my feet in Gainesville, I didn't have a job. I was working to become certified as a trainer, and Oprah's comments about my abs on national television had opened a door for me. Just days after the show aired, I received a phone call from Shelly Williams, the assistant to Jake Steinfeld, of "Body by Jake." Jake has always been one of my heroes so when she said Jake wanted to schedule a time for a conference call, I could hardly believe it. Shelly had been watching the Oprah show the day I was a guest and heard my comment about dreaming of becoming a personal trainer. The day Jake called I asked my husband and children to stay downstairs while I took the call. I sat and stared at the phone, bouncing around, staring at the phone, and waiting for it to ring. "Hello," I said, trying to sound upbeat and excited without sounding too silly. I pinched myself as Jake started talking to me. He was very friendly and said that if I had the guts to do what I did at my age, he was willing to give me a shot. He said "life was all about moments and this was one of my moments."

He challenged me to create a 10-minute ab routine and they would be in touch to help me schedule the when, where and details of the filming. I was going to have a spot on Exercise TV!

With no other job to go to, I jumped into planning the ab routine. But compared to the hectic pace of my life since I had moved to Gainesville, this was a really slow time in my life. I worked out a lot and went for long walks trying to make sense of everything and where I had been and where I was headed. I knew there was a lesson in all of this for me, and I wanted to make sure I learned it.

I questioned myself a lot during the quiet times of my day. Despite the confusion in the beginning, I didn't regret coming forward with my story. I felt liberated now that I wasn't lying any more. I saw a freedom in the children, too. Oprah had worried that my being on the show would cost my children their friendships, but to my knowledge, no one has abandoned my children or been cruel to them because they disapproved of me. To the contrary, most people have been very supportive. Even if they think stripping is morally wrong, people have not been unkind to any of us. In spite of all of my fears, people have amazed me. Not that some people might not be talking behind my back, but all-in-all, all of the friends who invited my children over for sleepovers before the truth came out, still invited them over after the show aired. They have taken the high road. From Shelly, my hairdresser, to Dawn and Scott at my church, people have continued to love me and be supportive of my children and family. Even my pastor, Dr. Tom Smiley and Robert Puckett, have been a huge encouragement to me. Dr. Tom's preaching has opened up my heart and mind to the joy and love of God and I have truly learned that when you are at the end of your rope is when you can get closer to God. For it's in our "brokenness" that we eventually become stronger in God.

Chapter 34 Going for it

It was a leap of faith when I finally decided to venture out and register for my personal training conference. I was putting action to a proposed dream and sometimes that can be just downright scary. I was nervous, but the overwhelming feeling was pure adrenaline and excitement. I got to the conference early on Saturday morning and got situated in my seat. Just then, Dr. Jack Barnathan walked in and began to speak. He talked about his passion for fitness and how we are to serve our clients. He told us that we always stick to the science of our profession and how to become invaluable to our clients by doing "the above and beyond...and then some." Not just being good or better, but being the best! His words were pure inspiration to me.

The moment he started talking I began to tear up. There I was, sitting in my seat at a personal training seminar at eight in the morning in full-fledged tears. But it wasn't just "any" seminar for me. It was a long-awaited step in a long-awaited dream. I thought of all of the time that had passed as I wanted to live out my dream instead of just dreaming my life away and this was the first step. It was liberating. It was empowering. It was then that this uncontrollable feeling came over me and what I would have to call an "Aha" moment and I just KNEW I was in the right place, at the right time, and for the right reason.

Dr. Jack couldn't help but notice my watery eyes, but he appreciated my passion. After the class was over, we talked at length. I began to tell him some of my story and he looked me square in the eyes and said, "You need to tell your story." I could tell that he meant what he said and in the months after that first initial meeting, and in the year that has passed since we first met, he has proven to be an added inspiration for me. He is so well-known and is so well respected for his knowledge, his service attitude, and his eloquence. His confidence in me gave me validation and has given me added courage to complete this book and strive even harder to become a Master Trainer and beyond.

Chapter 35 A healing

Even if you are not a person of faith, you have to admit that unforgiving people are hard to be around. Nothing is sadder than a bitter person bent on revenge. Maybe because I was always so aware of my own shortcomings, I've always understood the need for forgiveness for the "forgiver" and for the forgiven. The truth is, I was always so eager to please others most of my life, that I could never stay mad at anyone long enough to have to work too hard at forgiving anyone. I will confess, I did have to pray to find forgiveness for the man who abused me, but I thankfully never had to really struggle with deep bitterness towards him. Instead, I chose to concentrate on the positive and though he was not a good father, he had given me the 3 best gifts I could ever ask for: my children. Anything after that was pure gravy. I was just glad to be free of his reign over me and to be free of him.

I couldn't be mad at the Oprah staff for reporting what they saw: a single mom raising three children because in essence, that's exactly what I was, or what I had become. And in the end, I couldn't even be mad at Mick for not being able to give me what I most desired: a true, honorable, meaningful marriage. Mick had spoken from his heart from the very beginning and had given me all he knew he could. Some people have the gift of singleness and others - like I found myself to be - long for the special unification and sacredness of marriage. I ached to share even the sometimes "predictable" mundaneness of the "day in" and "day out" hustle and bustle of everyday life with my loving mate. Had I been totally honest in the beginning and spoken my heart's desire, instead of feeling like I wasn't worthy enough to expect God's best, I might have avoided a lot of my pain. Instead, I lived out of fear. I believed the lies that my ex husband had told me and I believed the adversary when those thoughts would creep into my mind and insist that "no one would ever want a woman with three children." I had decided the arrangement I had made with Mick was the best offer a girl like me could ask for. I so wanted to be loved that I settled for something far less than love and I almost lost myself in the process.

Knowing that, I just couldn't find any anger stewing inside of me when Mick couldn't live with and share a life with me and the children. He had to be true to himself and I finally had to be true to myself. I know he will be someone I can always turn to as a friend and I wish the very best for him. I believe he feels the very same way. And too, I firmly believe we left each other better than we found the other. He can now be who he needs to be and by my finally standing up for what I want and believe in, I have finally grown into the woman I have always wanted to be.

It wasn't until I began to take my children back to church and I began to study, really study, the Word that I began to see how I had shortchanged myself. From the beginning, the church opened its heart to me. The pastor, Dr. Tom Smiley, loved our family, even though he had no idea of the pain we had endured and were still in the midst of. I had thought for so long that God couldn't possibly still love me after all of my mistakes. It wasn't until I began to soak up every word of truth he spoke to his congregation that I began to realize that God had always loved me, He continues to love me, and will continue to love me regardless of my past or any future mistakes I may make. I began to not only learn the words of truth, but I began to "believe" them, and more importantly, live them.

One Sunday, Dr. Tom asked a very simple, but very direct question: "how has living outside of God's best worked out for you?" I squirmed in my chair. I'm sure there were others in the congregation that felt he was speaking to them, but I KNEW, without a shadow of a doubt, he was speaking straight at me.

I had to take a hard look at myself. I had not done life God's way, and it had cost me dearly. I knew that my family would never have the perfect situation where the mother and father stay together to share in raising and inspiring their children. For us, it was just never going to be that way. That's a hard pill to swallow and I ached not for me necessarily, but for my children. I knew that in my life, I had never made a complete surrender to God. I had always believed in God, but somehow I didn't believe the blessings the Bible talks about were for me. So in my experience, belief without faith doesn't hold much water. The good life, I thought, was for her or for him, not for me, and only until I grasped that God's best is for me, too, that I began to see myself differently.

I might not have been able to hold a grudge against other people who had hurt me in my life, but I was a champion at nursing anger towards myself.

So after a sincere prayer of confession, I began to do the long work of forgiving myself. That began with a list of things I wasn't proud of, but also included some of my greatest successes. I had kept my children together and I had kept my family intact. I had raised three children who are wonderful, talented, driven, and respectful children. No, they aren't perfect, anymore than any of us are, but they are each extraordinary individuals in their own way and they all love the Lord.

God continued to heal my heart as He taught me that all this time, as I had longed for intimacy with my partner(s), God had wanted that same deep intimacy with me. He wanted to comfort me, love me, and hold me close. He wanted to brush me off and send me back to myself whole and new. He used all of my experiences to show me that I needed Him, first and foremost, and then I would be prepared to handle whatever came my way. Furthermore, He gave me His commandments as protection for me, not to be a killjoy, as maybe I had sometimes perceived them to be. I began to see that the choices I had made were unhealthy because they weren't in line with God's best for me. The sad thing is, they weren't even what I had wanted. I gave up what I wanted and believed in to please other people in my life so that I could be accepted and gain what I thought was love.

Chapter 36 Priceless

I am in the blood of your heart
The breath of your lung
Why do you run for cover
You are from the dirt of the earth
And the kiss of my mouth
I have always been your lover

-Here I am, Emmy Lou Harris

Not long after the show aired, I saw an envelope among the bills that caught my eye. I was driving at the time, but in the stack I'd just collected from the mailbox was a letter from my dear friend, Winnie Long, "Gooey's" mom. I opened the letter, grateful to hear from her, but nervous that she might be disappointed in me. She had seen me on the Oprah show and not knowing my address, had sent her letter to my mom who had then forwarded it on to me. I pulled over to the side of the road to finish the letter which touched me deeply. With her permission, I've reprinted her note that you can find alongside the picture gallery.

Mrs. Winnie had always been important to me and with a newfound freedom in my schedule I decided to drive up to South Carolina to visit with her. I told her about my opening a private fitness studio and my passion to help people get into shape, take care of themselves and find the athlete within. Mrs. Winnie has a debilitating illness and to talk to me she had to point at letters to spell her words, but primarily we communicated with hugs, touches, and smiles. We visited for hours and then I got in my car to head home.

I took the long way home, stopping by the old swim center. As I walked in the doorway, I instantly remembered the smell of chlorine and saw that my name was still up on the record boards in a few events. I, smiled, too, when I saw our State Championship Trophy sitting proudly in the trophy case. It still felt good after all of these years to see that trophy and know I had played a part in that success.

It was very emotional day for me, and on the ride home I allowed my mind to drift from thought to thought with no real objective. I turned off the radio to give my mind the quiet it needed for processing the feelings and memories my visit to Mrs. Long and the old pool had stirred up.

Most of my life, I had run hard and fast from the dark thoughts that tried to overtake me. When something bad happened, I lifted my chin and made a plan to move on. I truly believe I always equated weakness as failure. I was almost as good at running from the deep rumblings as I was at swimming in my glory days. But as I headed back to Georgia, I knew that it was time I faced whatever was lurking down in the basement of my soul. I drove home slowly and tried to prepare myself for what I knew would be terribly painful. I had tasted what was coming before during the worst nights in the little concrete house. There were times when the only reason I didn't take my own life was because I could not leave my children alone in that hell. It was coming, that ugly darkness and I could feel it.

I barely remember most of the ride home, but I was so grateful for the goodness of Mrs. Long and the sweet memories of my successes in the pool. They helped me hold on. They were the anchor God had given me so I could withstand the swells in the coming storm.

Back home, I spent some time with the kids and then went out onto the back patio to stare at the stars. The night was cool but comfortable. Stars have always fascinated me. It's remarkable to me that they are always there, even in the daytime when the earth turns toward the sun and our eyes see the beautiful illusion of blue. The black infinity of the night sky speckled with powerful suns that are so far away that they are only specs of light puts me in my place. I am tiny and insignificant; and if I live to be 100, I am a nothing compared to the time and power of a star, but nevertheless, I am important to God. We all are.

"I can do this in small pieces," I told God. "If you can send it to me like the contractions of childbirth, I'll survive. But I need some breaks in between." With that simple prayer, I asked God to help me see the truth and really trust Him to take care of me when the dark pangs of guilt, shame, and loneliness crept in. My decisions to turn away from Him began to pierce me.

For the first time, I allowed myself to feel the horrible pain I had pushed down after my first marriage had failed. I had not permitted myself to fully grieve that experience before I had crawled into bed with the man who would become my captor. Sex with him was a way to make certain I didn't have to feel the ache of being alone. For a while, it worked. A new relationship medicated the pain of loneliness like a wonderful dream-inducing narcotic. But gaining the attention of a man did nothing to cure the real problem, the infection of emptiness that I had numbed but I had never acknowledged.

I cried as I thought of things I had done that must have broken God's heart. Excuses started to rise up inside me. They were familiar but I knew them for what they were. "Forgive me. Teach me," I whispered. I plunged my hands into the pocket of my sweater; and felt the collection of coins that the cashier had given me at the convenience store earlier that day. I couldn't see the coins in the darkness, but I knew them by the feel: one dime, a nickel and four pennies.

At once, I was overcome with fear: nineteen cents. "You're right back where you started, Marian," said the voice in my head. I was overcome with a wave of pain that shook my entire body. I thought of the nights I had felt so grateful, and yes, sometimes even powerful as men gave me $50 and $100 bills. I thought of the nights, too, where I was imprisoned and abused without a penny to my name. As my heart raced, my senses filled with the smell of alcohol, sweat and sex. I got up from the blanket that I'd spread on the cool concrete. I staggered back a step, caught my balance and stood like a statue, alone in the middle of the patio behind my home. The light was still on in Sydney's room. I then felt myself take a breath and realized how long I had held my breath and how desperately I needed to fill my lungs with air. Just as I thought I would be completely overcome, a soft breeze picked up just above the tree line and brought me the smell of something sweet: maybe honeysuckle, faint and wonderful. I turned my head toward the darkness of the trees trying to catch the sound of an echo I thought I had heard, but the whisper was gone. "Priceless," I think it said.

I bent over, picked up the coins that I had dropped on the concrete and stacked them largest to smallest in my hand. It wasn't even nineteen cents at all. I smiled and slid the money back into my pocket.

I felt a gentle calm that I have come to know as His presence. Like the stars, He's always there, even when illusions block my view. I walked slowly back toward the house with a rising strength.

I am still learning.

I am listening.

Lead me.

Guide me.

Chapter 37 Thank you

God, I thank you for not giving up on me. I thank you for chasing after me and finally wrestling me to the ground. I thank you for loving me and never giving up on me. Thank you.

A Special Tribute...

I have so many people to thank for their love and support. From the time when I can barely remember, to right now, I know, many times over, I have already met angels here on earth and your love and kindness has meant the world to me and has blessed my life beyond measure. I can only hope that I have been able to give back to each of you as much as you have given to me.

As for my children; Sydney, Hunter, and Dorothy, I love you all so much! Each of you, respectively, is the most wonderful child a mother could ask for and I am so very proud of each of you for standing strong in the face of adversity, and more importantly, for sticking up for each other all of these years. You each share in the amazing victory of keeping our family intact, strong, and happy. Your love and need for security has kept me going when I might have not had the strength to carry on, and your love and faith in me has kept me stronger than you may ever know. Your resilience of spirit never ceases to amaze me and I consider myself to be the lucky one to have had the privilege of being your mom. You are all still so young and the world is full of unknowns, but the one thing I have no reservation about is that I know you each possess the knowledge and determination to tackle any obstacle that may lie ahead of you. Your strength of character and self, unbridled by your deep-seeded faith will guide you into a most remarkable future. May you each grow up to be the wonderful adults that I know you are destined to become and may you always know how very much I love each one of you.

To my mom, I thank you for all of your advice, for never giving up on me, and for loving me no matter what. The older I get, the smarter YOU get, and I am proud to have a mom like you! To my dad, although you've been gone from my physical life since 1997, I thank you for your amazing love while you were with me here on earth, for continuing to love and support me from afar, and for cheering me on just like you always did. I can feel your presence, even though I can't see you, and it warms my heart to know that I was loved by you. To Sue and Beth, your courage to help a friend in need became my saving grace. You two have stood by me through thick and thin and I will never forget your love and faith in me. To Ellen and Jerry, your kindness and friendship to me and my children defies all limits. You both put new meaning in the phrase, "above and beyond." To Julie, you are, without a doubt, the coach of coaches. To Kristen, Sandy, and Stephanie, thanks for always listening and for all that you've done, and continue to do, to make my life just a little bit easier. To all of my clients, past and present, I am humbled and honored by your faith and trust in me. To Susan D., I couldn't have done this without you. Thank you for believing in me and my story. To Debbie and Donnie, your love and devotion to me and the children has stood the test of time. I read once that blood is thicker than water, but God is thicker than blood. I'm glad that is the case because we will always be family. To my sister Susan and my newly departed sister, Nancy, I thank you both for loving me and guiding me as only sisters can do. To my brother, Dave, thank you for opening up your home when we had nowhere else to go. You took my family in and made us feel important and loved and you've never given up on me or my potential. I will forever be indebted to you for your brotherly love and devotion.

About the Author

Marian Wardlaw was the youngest of four children born to Earle and Rebekah Wardlaw from Anderson, SC. She began swimming at the age of 6 and quickly rose to State Champion by the age of 8. Most of her early life was spent in the pool striving for excellence, studying hard in school, and working toward a college scholarship. In 1982, Marian's dream of earning that college scholarship became a reality. Despite her outward confidence and gregarious personality however, Marian struggled with her value as a woman and somehow developed a tendency to sell herself short, especially in relationships with men. In those dark times, instead of calling on her faith and looking to God for answers to her most sought after questions, Marian made decisions that left her life spiraling out of control and nearly shattered her once happy, fairy-tale life. At Marian's lowest point, with only 19Cents to her name, she questioned how she would ever be able to raise her three children in a happy and positive environment. Through sheer determination and the grace of God, Marian finally realized the root of her problem and began the long journey of rediscovering her unshakable spirit that had made her such a great champion in her youth. Marian currently resides with her three beautiful children in Georgia. With a newfound sense of freedom and vitality, today Marian is living her dream as a Certified Personal Trainer in her own fitness facility just North of Atlanta and through her Online Consulting Business. Marian coaches and inspires countless women, all over the country, in the areas of weight training, nutrition, positive attitude, and goal setting with the specific purpose to help others recapture their inner strength, confidence, and to live their best lives. Marian's website is www.marianwardlawfitness.com.